EXPLORING COLOUR
IN KNITTING

Techniques, swatches and projects to expand your knitting horizons

Sarah Hazell & Emma King

COLLINS & BROWN

To my mum – who taught me to knit.
To Jez, for his patience, encouragement and love.

First published in the United Kingdom in 2011 by
Collins & Brown
10 Southcombe Street
London W14 0RA

An imprint of Anova Books Company Ltd

ISBN 9781843405931

A CIP catalogue for this book is available from the British
Library.

10 9 8 7 6 5 4 3 2 1

Reproduction by Rival Colour UK Ltd
Printed and bound by Toppan Leefung, China

This book can be ordered direct from the publisher at
www.anovabooks.com

Contents

Introduction

As two knitters with a passion for colour, the opportunity to write a book about how colour is used in knitting has always been at the top of our wish list. As Rowan Design Consultants and Workshop Tutors we have also become aware of the dilemma that many knitters share – that of being drawn to the beautiful colours of yarns, but not feeling comfortable with putting them together or altering colour schemes. We were also conscious that unlike the artist who can mix colours to their own specification, knitters have to use what they are presented with, the shades that are current each season. And so the concept of exploring colour in knitting became the basis of this book. While we do, of course, recognize accepted colour theories, these are only referred to in the context of how this affects you the knitter, and not as a preferred way of working with colour.

The book is written for knitters of all skill levels, since it is primarily aimed at increasing your confidence and ability to work with colour. In Chapters 2 and 3 you will discover how different colour relationships and techniques can influence and impact on your choice of colour. Chapter 4 looks at how decorative elements can influence your perception of colour. The techniques of intarsia and Fair Isle are explored in chapters 5 and 6, with the emphasis being placed on how you can manipulate these techniques to achieve the results you are looking for: for example, how to change an existing colour scheme or how to build up a colour scheme for a Fair Isle pattern from scratch. The final chapter is there to act as a springboard for your own designs, demonstrating how to translate what has inspired you into a piece of knitted fabric. Each topic or chapter has an accompanying project to illustrate how theories can be put into practice. We hope that you will enjoy knitting these and then go on to produce your own interpretations of these designs.

We do not claim to have all the answers about how to use colour in your knitting. Choice of colour is a personal, often emotive subject, with external influences – such as fashion trends and cultural associations – playing their part. It is simply not appropriate to prescribe a set of rules to work from: instead we want you to use this book as source of inspiration as well as a reference point, so that you can test out what works for you.

In writing the book we have learnt so much and discovered many possibilities for working with colour ourselves. We have both been struck by how significant the interplay between yarn, stitch pattern and proportion is when using colour. In fact, we often found ourselves wanting to try out far more ideas than could ever be contained in one volume. And that is the opportunity we hope that this book will offer you – permission to test and discover all sorts of exciting possibilities!

Sarah Hazell & Emma King

1

What does colour do?

Being asked to respond to the question, 'What are your favourite colours?' is a tricky business. The response on any particular day may depend on a whole set of other circumstances, such as mood, trends and occasion. In this chapter we will start to answer this question by:

- giving a brief overview of colour production.

- looking at natural and synthetic dyes.

- acknowledging fashion and cultural influences.

- encouraging you to document and organize your own responses to colour.

- describing our personal responses to favourite colour palettes.

What is colour?

We need to look to the world of science to answer this question.
Put simply, colour is light.

Light can be divided up into seven different wavelengths and each of these wavelengths is a colour. These are the seven colours of the rainbow – red, orange, yellow, green, blue, indigo and violet.

When light comes into contact with an object, some of the wavelengths will be reflected back and some will be absorbed. This determines the colour that we see as our eye picks up the reflected light. This was famously discovered by Sir Isaac Newton in the 1640s and is the principle of how we are able to see colour.

Colour is all around us – every day we use colour to live our lives. Sometimes colour will affect us subconsciously, for example, we might have seen a red road sign that was warning us of a hazard ahead. On a conscious level, we might think about colour when we are deciding what to wear in the morning. Colour will matter to each and every one of us, several times a day.

Where do colours come from?

Colour is a very significant part of design and how colour is used in all aspects of art and craft, including knitting, is very important. Today, knitters have wide ranges of yarn colours to choose from, allowing us to create a wealth of different palettes, but this was not always the case.

Advancements have been made in the dyeing process over thousands of years. Dyeing was first recorded in the Bronze Age and right up until the mid-nineteenth century all dyes were taken from natural sources. The ancient Egyptians used madder to make red, woad to make blue and weld to make yellow. The Aztecs used the cochineal beetle to give them bright red and purpura shells to give them purple. The Vikings also used madder and woad, and went a step further by mixing them together to create a green. These natural sources were used to dye a variety of textiles.

In the 1850s, the first synthetic dye stuff called 'Mauveine' was discovered. The discovery was made by William Henry Perkin and the colour produced was a bright fuchsia. The next twenty years saw the discovery of synthetic dyes for brown, black and indigo. A synthetic version of madder was also produced, this being the first time a synthetic substitute had been created for a natural dye.

At the end of the nineteenth/beginning of the twentieth century, these gradual developments in dyeing, together with advances in the field of chemistry, saw a firm move to the synthetic production of colours. This ability to produce artificial dyes led to the creation of a broader range of colours.

It was this advancement that provides knitters with the wide range of shades available to them today. The yarns that we use vary in their construction and fibre content and these differences govern what sort of dyeing process each yarn goes through. Two common synthetic dye processes are reactive dyeing and acid dyeing.

Reactive dye was the first synthetic dye to react with the actual fibre itself and is often used for man-made fibres. The colour becomes part of the fibre rather than a separate element sitting on top of it. Reactive dyes allow us to create bright colour palettes and they also retain their colour fastness well.

Acid dyes are soluble and can be applied directly using a water/dye solution; they are often used for dying fibres such as wool and silk. As with reactive dyes, bright colours can be achieved by using acid dyes and they retain their colour fastness well against light, but not so well through washing.

The historical journey of the dyeing process has gone full circle with a return to natural dyes for organic yarns. Natural resources such as plant dyes are being used once again due to an increase in demand for organic and eco-friendly products.

Organically dyed yarns don't have to be dull, muted colours.

Fashion and cultural responses to colour

Scientific developments have resulted in manufacturers being able to create almost any colour they want. This wider availability of colours has resulted in colour being used increasingly as an indicator of fashion and cultural trends. However, historically colour has always been important in almost every aspect of life.

Clothing

Colour and fashion are intrinsically linked. The colours that we wear often reflect personality and impact both our emotions and other people's emotions – the colour of your clothing will often be the first thing somebody notices about you.

Different colours will go in and out of fashion and so, for example, in Western fashions different palettes can be linked to different eras. Black and white was popular in the 1920s, the 1940s saw the use of faded pastels and the fashions of the 1950s featured a lot of pink and turquoise. The 60s and 70s saw the widespread use of browns, oranges and avocado green.

The ability to link palettes to different eras is largely associated with social, economic and lifestyle trends at the time. Today, fashion houses and designers rely a great deal on the skills of colour forecasters who predict what the next themes will be. Forecasters around the world look to the future to see how various factors might be influencing consumer behaviour. Markets around the world will differ and successful interpretation of the trends within each market allows the forecasters to develop a range of colours suitable for that market's needs.

Colour palettes reflect current trends, including contemporary interpretations of vintage palettes.

Interior design

As with the colours of the clothes that we wear, the colours that we use to decorate our home will have a direct impact on our emotions, as well as reflecting our personality.

We associate colours with different feelings and we often consider this in interior design. For example, the kitchen, which is often the hub of activity in many houses, might be decorated in bright, bold colours to reflect that energy. In contrast, a bedroom might be painted in muted, tranquil colours to convey a more relaxed feel at the end of the day.

Some people are willing to take more risks with their colour scheme at home as opposed to the palette that they wear. There are people who absolutely love a colour such as orange but wouldn't wear it, though they are very happy to fill the living room with it!

The environment in which we live can also influence the colours that we choose to use in our homes. In Scandinavia, the long winters and reduced daylight hours mean that houses often have bright, open-plan interiors decorated in neutrals such as whites and creams to make optimum use of the natural light. In Northern European countries bright colours are sometimes perceived as loud and glaring, but in warmer countries where the sunlight is much stronger, the brighter, intense colours are needed.

Cultural meanings and associations

As we have already mentioned, colour impacts the day-to-day lives of everyone around the world. We all have our own personal responses to colour (turn to pages 16–17 for ours), and in addition to these there are cultural responses to colour that we must also consider.

We often associate colours with certain objects or feelings and these responses are often governed by our language and culture. This means that some colours will be perceived very differently around the world.

For example, Western cultures associate black with mourning, whereas in South Africa it is red, in Egypt it is yellow and purple is the colour of mourning for widows in Thailand. The Chinese associate red with good luck while Westerners usually associate luck with the colour green. In Eastern cultures, the bride often wears red on her wedding day and in Western cultures it is traditionally white.

The reasons for the wide range of differing associations can be linked to various things. Some will derive from political and historical matters, such as the colour of a country's flag or colours used by political parties. Some will stem from religious beliefs, where colours can have strong symbolic meanings, or there could be linguistic influences. These varying perceptions of colour and the importance placed on them highlights the power individual colours have and why colour is such an important factor of our lives.

How to start organizing your responses to colour

You may be somebody who already has an acute sense of colour in the world around you, or who is instinctively able to choose the 'right' colour in a given circumstance. You may be somebody who would like to feel more confident about introducing and experimenting with colour in your work. You probably find that there are times when your head is so full of colours and ideas that you feel it will explode, and then others when the ability to select and combine eludes you. Whatever point you have reached in your relationship with colour, the need to collect, record and reflect on your sources of inspiration is vital.

One of the best ways to organize your responses to colour is to keep a sketchbook. The kind of sketchbook that you choose to use will need to be personal to you and your requirements. As a knitter you will probably want to use it for storing swatches and so a loose-leaf file or storage box will usually be more appropriate than a bound book. Try to make sure that any notes or sketches in relation to these swatches are also easily accessible. Some designers choose to clip their swatches to the top of a page so that any additional information can be added as ideas develop.

Some of your best sources of inspiration may present themselves while you are out and about. So it is a good idea to have a camera with you at all times, as well as a notebook for recording your responses and making a quick sketch. Some galleries and museums do not allow you to take photographs so a notebook, as well as a visit to the gift shop for postcards, becomes essential.

A sketchbook does not have to be full of beautiful drawings! Instead, it should act more like a database and may contain notes, quotes, photographs, magazine tear sheets, swatches, scraps of thread and fabric, buttons, etc. Don't forget to add details as to where you found these sources of inspiration and why they were important to you at the time. As your sketchbook grows it will become a reference point and help you to clarify and develop your ideas. For example, referring back to a photograph may help you to identify an important element such as the proportion of colours to each other in a particular scheme.

A sketchbook is also a useful way of testing out your ideas. Use your sketchbook to create collages. Collage is a fantastic way of exploring how a colour scheme may work, before putting yarn onto the needles. Try covering a page with as many examples of one colour that you can find. This may include magazine tears, fabric scraps, buttons, yarn, paints, crayons, etc, and will help you to discover the enormous potential that individual colours have to offer. For example, a page of 'blue' will reveal a collection ranging from dark, murky indigos through to light, chalky pastel tones. Another useful way to test and record colour ideas is to cut a small rectangle of card and wrap yarns around it. Alter the proportion and order of the colours used to discover which is the most successful scheme.

As a knitter, your mantra must be – swatch, swatch, and swatch again! Use your yarn and needles to respond to the question, 'What if...?' 'What if I knit one row of purple and then three rows of turquoise, followed by a block of red?' 'What if I use larger needles than those recommended?' 'What if I blend several yarns together?' The permutations are, of course, endless, but that is what is so exciting about introducing colour into your knitting.

Always record details of the type and shade of yarn used along with needle size. What was it like to knit with and would you use it again? All of these responses will be useful when you start to put your ideas into practice.

A sketchbook is a personal database and you should fill it with whatever catches your eye.

Personal responses to colour

We all have one, or more, favourite colours. It's usually easy to tell a knitter's preferred colour, just have a quick look at their stash. There's bound to be a host of 'must-have' balls in a particular hue. We two have very different favourites, as you will see.

Sarah Hazell

Several years ago I signed up for a beginners' watercolour class. Amongst other things, this taught me to really look at the colours around me and not to assume that something would be a certain colour because it had always been so. I have continued to appreciate the myriad of colour combinations that we experience on a daily basis. But there is one group of colours that will always be my comfort zone and that is pinks and purples.

As you will discover when reading through the rest of the book, pink is not strictly a colour but is a tint of red. However, this does not limit its appeal or diversity. Pale, pastel shades are kind and forgiving and work well with almost any other colour. Deeper, more 'shocking' tones add vibrancy and sometimes present something of a challenge! Ultimately I feel comfortable with pink and am fascinated by the fact that it works so well in so many different situations and applications, from lipstick through to football shirts.

Purple is a close relation to pink since it is made from different combinations of red and blue. As with red, soft, pastel tints can be achieved by adding white, but it is the rich berry-like tones that I love the most. These also work well with lots of other colours. Purple is also something of a contradiction, being elegant, yet quite daring all at the same time. There is a line from a poem, 'When I grow old, I shall wear purple.' This expression of genteel defiance and a desire for independence sums up my feelings towards this colour, and in my dotage, I hope to still be wearing purple!

Emma King

The fact that Sarah and I have embarked on writing this book rightly suggests that I love colour – not just one or two colours, but all colours. I have many favourites, all for different reasons, but the two colours that really stand out for me are teal blues and greens – used independently and used together.

I'm not a fan of what I would call 'true blues' (which could be associated with my school uniform, which consisted of various shades of blue), but as soon as a blue is verging on the turquoise/teal, I love it! It is the addition of green that sends blue in the teal direction and so could this be linked to my love of green too?

As a magpie is attracted to all that glitters, if you put me in front of a display of yarn, I'll make a beeline for the teals and greens before anything else. If I try to think back to what might have triggered my love of these two colours, I have a vivid memory of a set of beautiful teal buttons in my Mum's sewing basket that I thought looked lovely on their card. I never had the desire to put them on anything – I just loved looking at them on the card.

Green is more of a mystery as I don't have a vivid memory associated with greens and think it's probably a colour I have come to admire more recently. If I had to choose which particular greens I am particularly fond of it would be limes and olives – the beautiful lime and olive greens that we see paired so often with fuchsia pinks and purples in contemporary palettes are just fantastic.

Teal is a very soothing colour. I think it is also very useful and extremely versatile as it can be put with many other colours and nearly always works well. Dark teals can be quite rich and elegant while lighter teals can be very pretty and delicate. We see green working well in nature everyday and so it makes sense that it, too, is good company for other colours.

2

Understanding colour

The aim of this chapter is to help you understand the various relationships that exist between different colours. We are not giving a set of rules, but simply helping you to gain confidence in your colour choices by:

– exploring the full potential of hue families.

– comparing warm and cool colours and their impact on a design.

– considering brights, pastels and neutrals as themes or accents.

– explaining the difference between complementary and analogous colour schemes and exploring how these choices might be modified.

– offering projects that translate concepts into knitted designs.

Techniques

The simplest colour knitting technique to learn is how to change yarn colours. Doing this the right way will make your knitting look better.

Joining in at the side

The technique for joining in a different-coloured ball of yarn on the edge of a piece of knitting is the same as that for joining in a new ball of the same colour in order to complete a project.

Carrying yarn up the side of the work

Working in stripes can create a lot of ends that need sewing in. Therefore it is a good idea to carry yarns up the side of the work to where you need them next, rather than cutting and rejoining all the time.

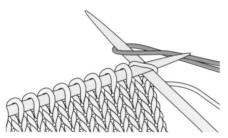

1 At the start of the row, insert the right-hand needle into the stitch as if to work it. Loop the new yarn around the tip of the needle, making sure the tail is about 15cm long.

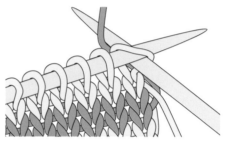

If you are only working two rows of each colour, it is fine to simply work the next row with the new colour. However, if you are working in wider stripes you must make sure you catch the yarn at the side of every alternate row – this stops big loops of yarn forming at the side. To catch the yarn, lay the yarn that you want to carry over the working yarn so that when you work the first stitch of the row, the carrying yarn gets caught.

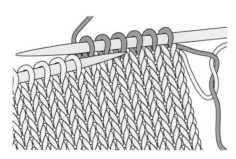

2 Work the next few stitches. To stop the stitches loosening, tie the ends of the new and old yarn together in a single knot. When the knitting is complete, unpick the knot and sew in the ends of yarn, making sure that each colour end is sewn into the back of stitches of the same colour. This helps prevent the wrong colour showing on the front of the work.

Joining in mid-row

Joining in a new colour on the row before you need it is a great way of reducing the number of ends that you will have to sew in once the project is finished.

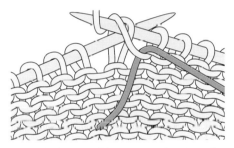

1 On the last row of the existing colour, stop about six stitches before the end of the row. Introduce the new colour by laying it over the existing colour. Support the tail end of the new yarn with your left thumb and work the next stitch in the existing colour, making sure you have caught the new yarn into the back of the stitch.

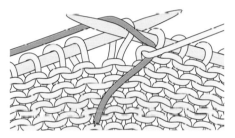

2 You can now work to the end of the row, weaving the new yarn into the back of the stitches as you go. Insert the right needle into the next stitch on the left needle and lay the new colour over the needle point.

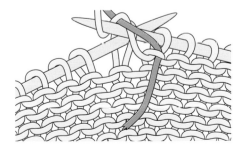

3 Using the existing colour, work the next stitch as normal, but as you work the stitch, lift the new yarn up and out of the way so that it doesn't form part of the stitch.

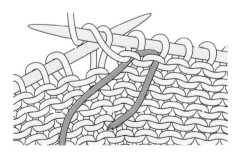

4 Step 3 placed the new yarn in such a way that working the next stitch as normal in the existing yarn will trap it, thereby carrying it across the back of the work. Repeat Steps 3–4 until you have reached the end of the row.

Colours and values

While you will certainly know what 'colour' means, you may not know the term 'value' in relation to colour. The value of a colour is basically how deep it is and you need to know this in order to get the most from your colour designs. Colours and values are both illustrated here with wheels.

Colour wheel

The colour wheel helps to clarify the relationship between colours and how different colours are made. It can help us to make sense of a colour scheme, but it should in no way dictate our colour choices. However, it is a very useful tool that we can all relate to.

Presented in two dimensions, it is really about the layering and subsequent nuances of colour. The colour wheel is underpinned by the principle that there are three primary colours – red, yellow and blue. Mixing primary colours in equal proportions creates secondary colours. So, red and yellow create orange, blue and yellow create green and red and blue create violet. The third layer (tertiary colours), is created when equal amounts of a primary and a secondary are mixed together – so yellow and green will create yellow-green and so on.

Adding black, white and grey will produce a range of tints, tones and shades of a pure colour. Adding a primary colour to one of the twelve colours on the wheel will sometimes alter a colour completely: for example, when blue is added to orange, grey is made.

Values wheel

This is a black and white or 'values' version of the colour wheel. Again, this is for your reference and will prove useful when trying to alter or balance out an existing scheme. This is because the range of greys helps you to see easily the contrast between two or more colours.

The value of a colour is determined by finding the grey that it sits closest to. Each grey on the scale is represented by a number describing the percentage of black that has been mixed with white to create that specific grey, with white at 0 per cent and black at 100 per cent. Not surprisingly, yellow has the lightest value on the wheel, with 90 per cent of its relative grey being made from white. By contrast, violet's relative grey is only 10 per cent white and 90 per cent black, making it the darkest colour on the wheel.

It is important to recognize the value of a colour, since this will be the first aspect of a design that the eye registers and the one it will retain for the longest.

Hue families

Hue is simply another name for colour. In practice it acts like a surname, allowing us to describe all of the variations of that colour within one segment of the colour wheel: spring green, grass green, and such like. Another name for a hue family is a 'monochromatic combination'.

For knitters, it is a useful exercise to gather together yarns from one hue family and knit up swatches to discover the effect that different members of the family have on one another. You will be amazed at how many different members of these families you find.

Four different hue families have been explored in the swatches shown here – greens, pinks, blues and browns. We have knitted the swatches starting with dark variations and working through to light. Knitting the swatches in this way allows you to see the variety of yarns available in a family.

Taking time to look at a particular hue family makes you realize just how many different variations of a colour there are, from brights through to duller colours. When choosing a colour or colours for a project you might already know that you want to use a particular colour – for example, pink – but which pink? Gathering together all the pinks available to you helps you to start forming an idea about exactly what you want.

It is possible to create a complex and interesting design using just one hue family – so understanding hue families allows you to add depth to a 'one-colour' project. Using a mixture of values – bright, dark and mid colours – allows you to create interest while working within one colour family. However, it is important to choose one of these values to be your main colour and then the others can be your accents.

Here we have chosen three greens – two are quite close in value (fairly dark) and the third is a lot lighter. The darker values dominate and the lighter value acts as a welcome highlight. The fact that all these colours are from the same hue family helps to ensure a pleasing result.

A hue family can also be a good base to add other colours to. For example, a green hue family would act as a great foundation for the occasional flash of pink or purple.

Here you can see the green family with pink added, which is actually its complementary. It is worth noting that it is very often effective to use a hue family as a base for accents of its complementary colour.

Hue family bag

Creating a palette from one hue family has allowed us to combine different textures, as the various pinks have been taken from different yarn ranges. A band of mid, dark and light pinks worked in a slip stitch stripe tops off the shaped bag. The pink lining ensures that the hue family theme is carried throughout the project.

MATERIALS

Three 50g/113m balls of DK yarn in dark pink (A)

One 25g/210m ball of 4-ply yarn in hot pink (B),
    used double throughout

One 50g/85m ball of DK yarn in sugar pink (C)

One 50g/125m ball of DK yarn in dusky pink (D)

Pair of 4mm knitting needles

Eight stitch markers

Knitter's sewing needle

Two pieces of lining fabric, each measuring 43 x 29cm

Sewing machine

Sewing thread

Sewing needle

Two pieces of wadding, each measuring 41 x 27cm

TENSION

22 sts and 30 rows to 10cm using 4mm needles
    measured over st st.

FINISHED SIZE

Circumference approx 82cm at widest point.

ABBREVIATIONS

See page 158.

Front and Back (both alike)

Using yarn A, cast on 26 sts.

Row 1: Knit.

Row 2: Purl.

Place a stitch marker on the 3rd, 6th, 9th, 12th, 15th, 18th, 21st and 24th sts: you should have eight stitch markers in total.

Row 3: [K2, m1, knit marked st, m1] to last 2 sts, k2. *(42 sts)*

Row 4: Purl.

Row 5: Knit.

Row 6: Purl.

Row 7: K3 [m1, knit marked st, m1, k4] to last 4 sts, m1, knit marked stitch, m1, k3. *(58 sts)*

Row 8: Purl.

Row 9: Knit.

Row 10: Purl.

Rep last two rows twice more.

Row 15: K4 [m1, knit marked st, m1, k6] to last 5 sts, m1, knit marked stitch, m1, k4. *(74 sts)*

Row 16: Purl.

Row 17: Knit.

Row 18: Purl.

Rep last two rows four more times.

Row 27: K5 [m1, knit marked st, m1, k8] to last 6 sts, m1, knit marked stitch, m1, k5. *(90 sts)*

Row 28: Purl.

Row 29: Knit.

Row 30: Purl.

Rep last two rows eight more times.

Row 47: K4 [skpo, knit marked st, k2tog, k6] to last 9 sts, skpo, knit marked st, k2tog, k4. *(74 sts)*

Row 48: Purl.

Row 49: Knit.

Row 50: Purl.

Rep last two rows four more times.

Row 59: K3 [skpo, knit marked st, k2tog, k4] to last 8 sts, skpo, knit marked st, k2tog, k3. *(58 sts)*

Row 60: Purl.

Row 61: Knit.

Rep last two rows once more.

Row 64: Purl, dec 1 st in the centre of this row *(57 sts)*

Change to yarn C.

Row 65: K1 [yfwd, sl1, ybk, k1] to end.

Row 66: Purl.

Row 67: K2 [yfwd, sl1, ybk, k1] to last st, k1.

Row 68: Purl.

Change to yarn B.

Row 69: K1 [yfwd, sl1, ybk, k1] to end.

Row 70: Purl.

Change to yarn D.

Row 71: K2 [yfwd, sl1, ybk, k1] to last st, k1.

Row 72: Purl

Row 73: K1 [yfwd, sl1, ybk, k1] to end.

Row 74: Purl

Change to yarn C.

Row 75: K1 [yfwd, sl1, ybk, k1] to end.

Row 76: Purl.

Row 77: K2 [yfwd, sl1, ybk, k1] to last st, k1.

Row 78: Purl.

Change to yarn B.

Row 79: K1 [yfwd, sl1, ybk, k1] to end.

Row 80: Purl.

Change to yarn D.

Row 81: K2 [yfwd, sl1, ybk, k1] to last st, k1.

Row 82: Purl.

Row 83: K1 [yfwd, sl1, ybk, k1] to end.

Row 84: Purl.

Change to yarn C

Row 85: K2 [yfwd, sl1, ybk, k1] to last st, k1.

Row 86: Purl.

Row 87: K1 [yfwd, sl1, ybk, k1] to end.

Row 88: Purl.

Change to yarn B.

Row 89: Knit.

Row 90 (WS): Knit (this forms the fold line).

Change to yarn A.

Row 91: Knit.

Row 92: K1, purl to last st, k1.

Rep last two rows twice more, ending with a WS row.

Cast off.

Handle (make 2)

Using yarn A, cast on 9 sts.

Row 1 (RS): Knit.

Row 2: Purl.

Rep last two rows until work measures 40cm from cast on
edge, ending with a WS row.

Cast off.

To finish

Darn in all loose ends neatly.

Sew the Front and Back together, sewing down one side,
across the base and up the other side.

FABRIC LINING

Using the knitted bag as a template, cut two pieces of lining
fabric slightly larger than the knitted pieces, plus 1cm at the
sides and base for the seam allowance. Machine sew the
two pieces together, sewing down one side, across the base
and up the other side. Turn the knitted bag inside out and with
the lining fabric also inside out, sew the bottom two corners of
the lining to the bottom two corners of the knitted bag. Fold
the lining back over the bag and it will look as if the whole
bag has been turned inside out.

Insert the pieces of wadding in between the knitted bag
and the fabric lining. Slip stitch the lining into place around
the top edge (catching the wadding at the same time). Fold
the top of the bag over at the fold line (row 90) and slip stitch
the cast off edge to the lining. Turn the bag the right way out.

Sew handles inside top of bag approx 2cm in from each
side seam, lining the cast on and cast off edges up with the
cast off edge of the knitted bag.

Warm and cool colours

In conversation, we often find it useful to describe colours to each other in terms of temperature, referring to warm reds, oranges and yellows as opposed to cool blues and greens.

Warm colours are generally recognized as red-violet, red, red-orange, orange, yellow-orange, and yellow.

Cool colours move from violet through, blue-violet, blue, blue-green, green to yellow–green.

The heat of warmer colours usually increases with added colour strength or intensity.

Cooler colours appear even chillier when white is added.

Warm colours are lighter in value than cooler ones, meaning that the ratio of lightness to darkness within these colours is likely to be at least 50 per cent, and in the case of yellow, more than 90 per cent. It is also important to realize that 'lighter' colours are retained by the eye for longer and 'read' first; in other words, their effect will stay with us for longer.

When a design is evaluated, most people agree that warm colours tend to advance or dominate, whereas cool ones tend to recede or give a greater feeling of distance. Careful selection of warm and cool colours can help you to create a three-dimensional effect in your work. Notice what happens when the warm pink and cool green swap places with each other in the square-within-a-square swatches on the left.

This has several implications for planning or altering a design. Even in small amounts, warmer colours will dominate, which means that if you want to achieve overall balance in your colour scheme, you should consider giving a larger area to cooler colours.

If you feel the need to cool down a warm colour – such as the orange shown in the middle band on the right – try to find an alternative to adding black, as this will simply overwhelm the colour, as shown in the lower band. You will find that adding the lightest of the cool colours – yellow-green in the top band – will temper a warm colour more successfully.

If your cool colours are too chilly – as with the green in the middle band on the far right – they can be warmed with yellow (top band), as opposed to white (lower band). Adding white will only tone down or present a pastel version of the colour and not necessarily make it any warmer.

Undertones

Unlike the artist, the knitter is always working with predetermined colours. Pigments used in the dyeing process mean that we are rarely knitting with 'pure' colours.

The colours that we are presented with will often carry their own undertone. An undertone is the small amount of warmth that you might find in a cool colour, or coolness that you might find in a warm colour. While this is never enough to change the overall characteristic of a given colour, it will have an impact, especially when surrounded by other colours or alongside other members of its hue family.

In the swatch above left you can see the contrast between a warm colour and a warm colour with a cool undertone. A minute amount of blue moves the colour on the right of the swatch to the purple side of red.

In the swatch on the right, a warmer undertone is contrasting with a cool colour, pulling the direction of the colour back towards red on the colour wheel.

'The mix of cool and warm undertones in the swatch on the left makes the stripes look harsh and visually unbalanced.'

An awareness of how these undertones can influence the surrounding colours in a design will help us to make the most successful choices. A piece of knitting that combines warm and cool undertones (above) is likely to be quite uncomfortable, whereas all warm (right) or all cool (below) undertones will increase the likelihood of the combination working more harmoniously.

Warm and cool throw

The idea of wrapping up against the cold was the inspiration behind using warm and cool colours in this throw. The cool purple and warm red are used in equal measure and are further balanced by warm ochre shades and cooler lime, lilac and dark green.

MATERIALS

Six 50g/113m balls of DK yarn in rich red (A)

Six 50g/113m balls of DK yarn in purple (B)

Two 50g/113m balls of DK yarn in dark green (C)

Two 50g/113m balls of DK yarn in lime green (D)

Two 50g/113m balls of DK yarn in gold (E)

One 25g/210m ball of 4ply silk/mohair yarn in
    lime green (F)

One 25g/210m ball of 4ply silk/mohair yarn in lilac (G)

One 25g/210m ball of 4ply silk/mohair yarn in gold (H)

Pair of 4mm knitting needles

Knitter's sewing needle

TENSION

22 sts and 30 rows to 10cm using 4mm needles
    measured over st st.

FINISHED SIZE

106 x 127cm.

ABBREVIATIONS

See page 158.

Panel A (make two)

Using yarn B, cast on 54 sts.

Row 1: P2, [k8, p6] to last 10 sts, k8, p2.

Row 2: Purl.

Row 3: As row 1.

Row 4: P1, k2, p6, [k2, p4, k2, p6] to last 3 sts, k2, p1.

Row 5: K2, p2, [k4, p2, k6, p2] to last 8 sts, k4, p2, k2.

Row 6: P3, k2, p2, [k2, p8, k2, p2] to last 5 sts, k2, p3.

Row 7: K4, P4, [k10, p4] to last 4 sts, k4.

Row 8: As row 6.

Row 9: As row 5.

Row 10: As row 4.

Rep rows 1–10 until work measures 45cm.

Cast off.

Panel B (make two)

Using yarn A, cast on 54 sts and work the following stripe
     sequence in st st.

Rows 1–3: A.

Rows 4–5: E.

Row 6: A.

Rows 7–9: E.

Rows 10–11: A.

Row 12: E.

Row 13: A.

Rows 14–15: E.

Row 16: A

Row 17: E.

Rows 18–19: A.

Rows 20–22: E.

Row 23: A.

Rows 24–25: E.

Rows 26–28: A.

Work should measure 9cm.

Cast off

Panel C (make two)

Using yarn F used double throughout, cast on 55 sts.

Row 1: K1, [p1, k1] to end.

Rep row 1 until work measures 15cm.

Cast off.

Panel D (make two)

Using yarn A, cast on 60 sts.

Row 1: [Sl1 purlwise, k2, psso, k3] to end.

Row 2: [P4, yrn, p1] to end.

Row 3: [K3, sl1 purlwise, k2, psso] to end.

Row 4: [P1, yrn, p4] to end.

Rep rows 1–4 until work measures 35cm.

Cast off.

Panel E (make two)

Using yarn D, cast on 54 sts.

Row 1: Knit in D.

Row 2: Purl in D.

Row 3: Knit in D.

Row 4: Purl in C.

Row 5: Knit in H.

Row 6: As row 5.

Rep rows 1–6 six more times and then rows 1–3 once more.

Next row: Purl in D.

Work should measure 15cm.

Cast off.

Panel F (make two)

Using yarn E, cast on 54 sts.

Row 1: Knit in E.

Row 2: Purl in E.

Row 3: Knit in H.

Row 4: Purl in H.

Rep rows 1–4 thirteen more times and then rows 1–2
     once more.

Work should measure 19cm.

Cast off.

Panel G (make two)

As Panel D, but rep rows 1–4 until work measures 50cm.

Cast off.

Panel H (make two)

As Panel F, but substituting yarn C for yarn E and yarn G for
  yarn H.

Panel I (make two)

As Panel C, but working in yarn G until work measures 10cm.

Panel J (make two)

Using yarn C, cast on 54 sts.

Row 1: K2, [p2, k4] to last 4 sts, p2, k2.

Row 2 and foll 2 alt rows: Purl.

Row 3: As row 1.

Row 5: K5, [p2, k4] to last st, k1.

Row 7: As row 5.

Row 8: Purl.

Rep rows 1–8 eight more times and then rows 1–4 once more.

Work should measure 25cm.

Cast off.

To finish

Darn in all loose ends neatly.

Press Panels B, E and F according to ball band
instructions.

STRIPS 1 AND 3

Using mattress stitch (or backstitch if preferred), sew cast off
edge of B to cast on edge of A, cast off edge of C to cast on
edge of B, cast off edge of D to cast on edge of C and cast
off edge of E to cast on edge of D.

STRIPS 2 AND 4

Sew cast off edge of G to cast on edge of F, cast off edge of
H to cast on edge of G, cast off edge of I to cast on edge of
H and cast off edge of J to cast on edge of I.

Again using mattress stitch (or backstitch if preferred),
sew strip 2 to 1, 3 to 2 and 4 to 3, ensuring that blocks are
aligned and using the photograph as a guide.

BORDER

TOP AND BOTTOM EDGES

With right side facing and yarn B, pick up and knit 190 sts
along top edge.

Work 1 row in moss st.

Continue in moss st and inc 1 st at each end of next and
foll 5 alt rows, ending with a RS row.

Cast off in pattern on WS.

Rep along bottom edge.

SIDE EDGES

Rep as for top and bottom, but picking up 254 sts along
row edges.

Join mitred corners using mattress stitch.

Brights

These are the colours that often provoke the most reaction, with people either loving them or loathing them! For some, these colours are cheerful and invigorating; to others they are a harsh reminder of all that was awful about fashion in the 1980s. Put quite simply, they are colour in its purest form with nothing added or taken away.

It is easier to decide how bright, or 'saturated', a colour is when that colour is compared to other members of its hue family. The saturated colour in the central stripe on the swatches above stands out more than those stripes that are less saturated.

A design that uses lots of colours of the same level of brightness may be too overpowering. It is usually a good idea at this stage to refer back to the hue family swatch you have made to see if there are different levels of brightness that you can use. This will have a similar effect to tinting, toning and shading. In other words, working two or more different colours with different levels of brightness will make the brighter one look brighter and the duller ones, duller.

There are several ways you can highlight a favourite bright colour. Try combining a bright with a pastel, the effect will be softer, but the pastel will tend to dominate because of its white content. The lighter the colour, the longer it will be retained by the eye.

It may be better to combine a bright with a neutral, which, in the same way as using different members of the same hue family, has the effect of making the bright more vibrant.

Even in small amounts, a bright will dominate or 'sing' out against a duller background.

Pastels

The easiest way to describe a pastel colour is that it is a colour that has had white added to it. Any colour can be a pastel – just add white!

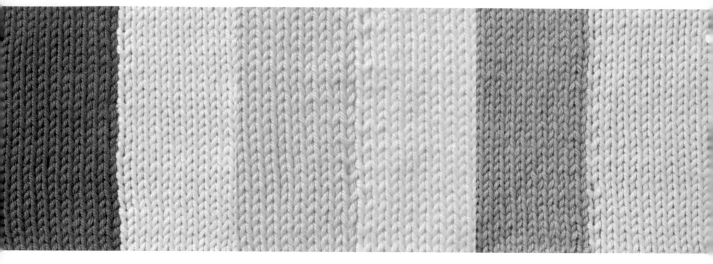

The swatches here show a bright pink, a yellow and a blue together with their pastel.

Pastels are often described as pale, delicate, soft or muted. This is because they are a watered-down version of a stronger colour. We tend to associate pastels with babies (baby pink and baby blue), and pastel colours can also make you think of sweets – candy shades such as a sugary pink, mint green or lemon yellow.

'A palette composed entirely of pastels might just work for a project for a small child, but is likely to look inappropriate in a project for an adult or an interior.'

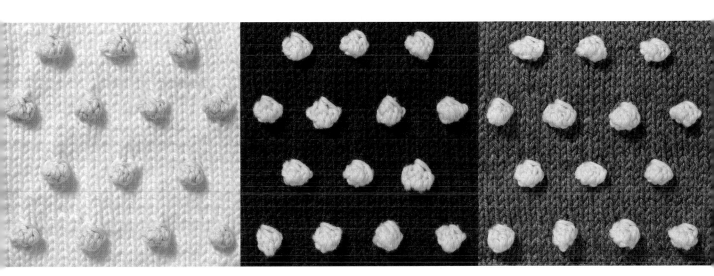

When using pastels in a palette, care must be taken to ensure that you do not create a palette that is too washed out. Combining pastels with neutrals is often a successful way of balancing a pastel palette, as long as the value of the neutral is right. A neutral that is too light won't provide enough contrast and a neutral that is too dark will be severe. get the value of the neutral right and you will have produced a pleasing combination.

These swatches use just one pastel pink and a neutral. The first swatch shows the pastel against a white background, which makes the pastel appear washed out. The second shows the pastel against a black background, which is too strong a contrast. The third swatch is a lot more successful as the value of the grey sits in between the white and black and complements the pastel shade, enhancing it.

Neutrals

If we look up the word 'neutral' in the dictionary, we find words such as 'indistinct', 'vague', 'not strong' used to describe it. All of these descriptions are quite negative, but as a colour, a neutral can be really very useful. Black, white, grey, cream, brown and beige are all what we would describe as neutral colours.

There are many different variations of a neutral; for example, when looking for a grey ball of yarn you will probably have to decide between various light greys, several dark greys and mid greys, too. All these different neutrals have their uses, as they will affect the colours around them, and vice versa, in different ways.

 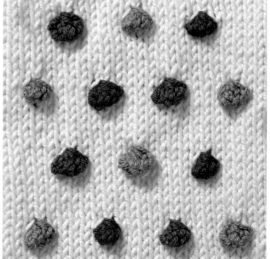

Neutrals make good backgrounds for other colours and can be used to consolidate colour palettes. In these two swatches pink, purple and green bobbles have been worked against two different backgrounds: the swatch on the left shows them on a coloured background (teal) and the one on the right on a neutral background (cream).

Three colours have been used for the bobbles and so the teal background is a fourth colour. The introduction of a fourth colour means there is an additional colour relationship for the eye to read and it's difficult to know what to look at first – the bobbles or the background? The eye keeps jumping around. Whereas when you look at the swatch with the neutral background, your eye focuses on the bobbles.

You will also notice that the colours of the bobbles have been affected by the teal background and they appear darker, but the neutral cream background allows you to view them in their natural state.

The other aspect of a neutral that is worth noting is that it can be a great antidote to a perhaps too powerful palette. The swatches above show two very bright colours worked in stripes – one has a neutral worked alongside the colours and the other hasn't. The neutral provides relief and a place for the eye to rest.

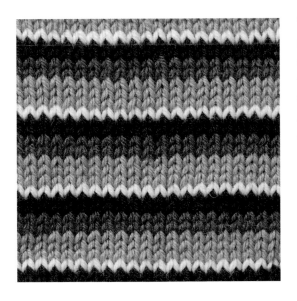

You must not forget that you can create interesting palettes from just neutrals – you don't always need to add colour. For example, this swatch shows a palette of two greys, black and white. The four neutrals vary in value from dark through to light and the depth that this combination creates is what makes the swatch interesting. If we had worked the swatch in neutrals of a similar value, it would not have been so successful.

Black

First of all, is black a colour? A scientist would perhaps argue that it isn't, but we are more than happy to class it as a neutral colour. You do need to be careful how you employ black within a palette, but used correctly it can be effective.

Black doesn't work well if used with very dark colours. It has the effect of dulling them, leading to a very dark, uninteresting palette. In this swatch the black does nothing to help the dark mulberry and olive.

However, if you put black with very bright colours, it serves to make them appear even brighter, bringing a palette to life. This is because black is the darkest neutral and so when paired with something as contrasting as a bright, it jumps out.

White

Again we ask the question – is it a colour? Well, this time a scientist would perhaps argue that it is. As with all neutrals it is a good background colour, but white is perhaps one of the most powerful neutrals as even when you use it in very small amounts it can still dominate a palette.

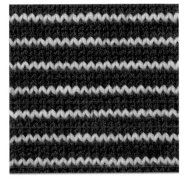

The swatch on the left shows equal stripes of purple and white, but even though equal proportions of each colour have been used, the white dominates.

The swatch on the right shows unequal stripes of the same colours and this time the white has been used in a far smaller proportion and yet, it still dominates.

This makes white a great highlight. The occasional stitch or rows of white can be just enough to lift a design.

Brown

Brown is one of the darker neutrals, but as it's not as dark as black it is a bit softer and so very useful for warming up palettes.

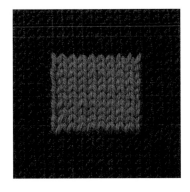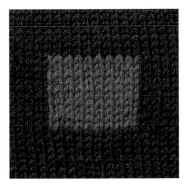

The swatch on the left shows a raspberry pink set against a black background and the swatch on the right shows the same pink set against a brown background. The pink appears a lot richer on the right. If you wanted to soften a palette whose neutral was black, consider using a brown instead.

Beige

Beige is a lighter version of brown and can serve a similar purpose in warming up palettes. For example, beige is a great way of adding warmth to a palette of cool blues.

The swatch on the left shows stripes of three cool blues; it works quite well but it is definitely cool in its overall appearance. The swatch on the right is the same sequence of blues but with a very occasional single row of beige added, which creates an instantly warmer feel.

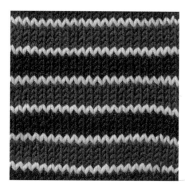

Beige is also very useful for accentuating darker colours. The swatch on the left shows equal stripes of a dark mulberry colour and a dark olive green; both colours are struggling to stand out. The swatch on the right uses a single row of beige to separate the colours, showing off both shades to their full potential.

The dark mulberry and olive used here were also used for the swatch exploring black on page 44. You might find it useful to compare what a difference the addition of beige has made in comparison to the black.

Grey

Like all neutrals, grey is a very good background colour. It is also a great substitute for other neutrals. A dark grey can be used instead of black and a light grey can be useful as a replacement for white. We have already seen how effective grey can be when teamed with pastels (page 41) and it can also be very useful if you want to cool down a warm palette.

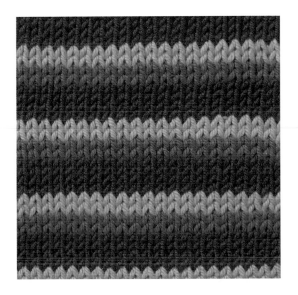

The swatch on the left uses stripes of three very warm reds and oranges. It works well, but if you wanted to cool it down the swatch on the right shows how introducing an occasional single row of grey does exactly that.

'The many shades of grey available in yarns gives the knitter lots of options with this useful neutral.'

Neutrals table runner

This project explores further the idea of creating a colour palette just from neutrals. Here we have looked at brown and how different tints, tones and shades of it can be put together to produce a well-balanced palette. The cream and beige dominate while the darker brown, combined with the beige, frames the design.

MATERIALS

One 50g/85m ball of DK yarn In chocolate brown (A)

Five 50g/85m balls of DK yarn in cream (B)

Two 50g/85m balls of DK yarn in beige (C)

Pair of 4mm knitting needles

Cable needle

Knitter's sewing needle

TENSION

21 sts and 28 rows to 10cm using 4mm needles
    measured over moss stitch.

FINISHED SIZE

Width: 26cm.

Length: 137cm.

ABBREVIATIONS

C6B = Cable six back: slip the next 3 sts onto cable
    needle and hold at back of work, k3 from left needle
    and then knit the 3 sts from the cable needle.

C6F = Cable six front: slip the next 3 sts onto cable
    needle and hold at front of work, k3 from left needle and then
    knit the 3 sts from the cable needle.

See also page 158.

Table runner

FIRST END SECTION

Using yarn A, cast on 60 sts.

Change to yarn B.

Rows 1–2: Knit.

Change to yarn A

Row 3: Knit.

Row 4: K3, purl to last 3 sts, k3.

Change to yarn C.

Rows 5–6: Knit.

Change to yarn A.

Row 7: K9, slip 2 sts [k6, slip 2 sts] to last 9 sts, k9.

Row 8: K3, p6, slip 2 sts [p6, slip 2 sts] to last 9 sts, p6, k3.

Change to yarn C.

Row 9: K9, slip 2 sts [k6, slip 2 sts] to last 9 sts, k9

Row 10: Knit.

Change to yarn A.

Row 11: Knit.

Row 12: K3, purl to last 3 sts, k3.

Change to yarn C.

Rows 13–14: Knit.

Change to yarn A.

Row 15: K5, slip 2 sts [k6, slip 2 sts] to last 5 sts, k5.

Row 16: K3, p2, slip 2 sts [p6, slip 2 sts] to last 5 sts, p2, k3.

Change to yarn C.

Row 17: K5, slip 2 sts [k6, slip 2 sts] to last 5 sts, k5.

Row 18: Knit.

Change to yarn A.

Row 19: Knit.

Row 20: K3, purl to last 3 sts, k3.

Change to yarn C.

Rows 21–22: Knit.

Change to yarn A.

Row 23: K9, slip 2 sts [k6, slip 2 sts] to last 9 sts, k9.

Row 24: K3, p6, slip 2 sts [p6, slip 2 sts] to last 9 sts, p6, k3.

Change to yarn C.

Row 25: K9, slip 2 sts [k6, slip 2 sts] to last 9 sts, k9.

Row 26: Knit.

Change to yarn A.

Row 27: Knit.

Row 28: K3, purl to last 3 sts, k3.

Change to yarn B.

Rows 29–30: Knit.

Change to yarn C.

Rows 31–32: Knit.

CENTRE SECTION

Now work using the intarsia technique (see pages 110–112) as follows:

Row 33: Using yarn B p1 [k1, p1] eleven times, k1, p2, using yarn C k1, m1 [k2, m1] three times, k1, using yarn B p2, k1 [p1, k1] to last st, p1. *(64 sts)*

Row 34: Using yarn B p1 [k1, p1] eleven times, p1, k2, using yarn C k12, using yarn B k2, p1 [p1, k1] to last st, p1.

Row 35: Using yarn B p1 [k1, p1] eleven times, k1, p2, using yarn C k12, using yarn B p2, k1 [p1, k1] to last st, p1.

Row 36: As row 34.

Row 37: Using yarn B p1 [k1, p1] eleven times, k1, p2, using yarn C C6B, C6F, using yarn B p2, k1 [p1, k1] to last st, p1.

Row 38: As row 34.

Row 39: As row 35.

Row 40: As row 34.

Row 41: As row 35.

Row 42: As row 34.

Row 43: Using yarn B p1 [k1, p1] eleven times, k1, p2, using yarn C C6F, C6B, using yarn B p2, k1 [p1, k1] to last st, p1.

Row 44: As row 34.

Row 45: As row 35.

Row 46: As row 34.

Rows 35–46 form the cable pattern. Rep these twelve rows until work measures 128cm from the cast on edge, ending with a row 45.

Next row: Using yarn B p1 [k1, p1] eleven times, p1, k2, using yarn C [p1, p2tog] four times using yarn B k2, p2, [k1, p1] to end. *(60 sts)*

SECOND END SECTION

Change to yarn C.

Next row: Knit.

Next row: Knit.

Change to yarn B.

Next row: Knit.

Next row: Knit.

Change to yarn A.

Next row: Knit.

Next row: K3, purl to last 3 sts, k3.

Change to yarn C.

Next row: Knit.

Next row: Knit.

Change to yarn A.

Next row: K9, slip 2 sts [k6, slip 2 sts] to last 9 sts, k9.

Next row: K3, p6, slip 2 sts [p6, slip 2 sts] to last 9 sts, p6, k3.

Change to yarn C.

Next row: K9, slip 2 sts [k6, slip 2 sts] to last 9 sts, k9.

Next row: Knit.

Change to yarn A.

Next row: Knit.

Next row: K3, purl to last 3 sts, k3.

Change to yarn C.

Next row: Knit.

Next row: Knit.

Change to yarn A.

Next row: K5, slip 2 sts [k6, slip 2 sts] to last 5 sts, k5.

Next row: K3, p2, slip 2 sts [p6, slip 2 sts] to last 5 sts, p2, k3.

Change to yarn C.

Next row: K5, slip 2 sts [k6, slip 2 sts] to last 5 sts, k5.

Next row: Knit.

Change to yarn A.

Next row: Knit.

Next row: K3, purl to last 3 sts, k3.

Change to yarn C.

Next row: Knit.

Next row: Knit.

Change to yarn A.

Next row: K9, slip 2 sts [k6, slip 2 sts[to last 9 sts, k9.

Next row: K3, p2, slip 2 sts [p6, slip 2 sts] to last 5 sts, p2, k3.

Change to yarn C.

Next row: K9, slip 2 sts [k6, slip 2 sts] to last 9 sts, k9.

Next row: Knit.

Change to yarn A.

Next row: Knit.

Next row: K3, purl to last 3 sts, k3.

Change to yarn B.

Next row: Knit.

Next row: Knit.

Change to yarn A.

Next row: Knit.

Cast off on WS.

To finish

Darn in all loose ends neatly.

Tints, tones and shades

The relationship between colours can also be altered or influenced by tinting, toning or shading them.

These swatches show what happens to a colour when you add white (tinting), grey (toning) and black (shading). While it is not possible to completely 'fuse' the colours of two yarns, we have used silk and mohair mix yarns combined with a textured stitch, such as moss stitch, to give the illusion of the yarns blending. This is a great technique to use when exploring the many possibilities a single yarn or colour can offer and is called 'optical mixing'. You can experiment with heavier-weight yarns, but the effect will be less regular and not so marled.

The original colour is on the left. Adding white gives a lighter, more pastel version of that colour. We can say that pink is a tint of red because it is made by mixing red and white together. Adding grey to a colour usually makes it appear duller, but will only alter the 'value' of that colour if it is a lighter or darker grey than the colour it is combined with. Consequently, tones are useful for calming rather than altering a colour more profoundly. Inevitably, adding black to a colour will make it darker and should probably be used sparingly! You will also need to consider its impact on the colours surrounding it.

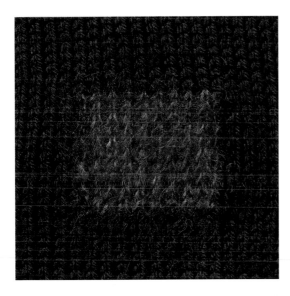

Background colour will also affect our perception of how dark or light a tone appears. Against a black background, the 'tone' appears more vibrant. Whereas, against the white one, it appears duller.

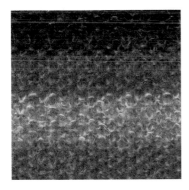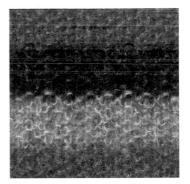

Similarly the order in which tints, tones and shades are placed alongside each other will need to be considered, as the changes in the colour values will be more pronounced in some sequences than others. Where tints and shades are placed alongside each other, there is more contrast than when a tone is used.

Tints, tones and shades snood

A snood is a great way to demonstrate the subtle interplay between the tints, tones and shades of a single colour. The bands of solid teal help to illustrate how much impact adding black and white to a colour can have. The toning effect of adding grey is less noticeable and produces a colour closer to the original.

MATERIALS

Two 25g/210m balls of 4ply silk/mohair yarn in teal (A)
One 25g/210m ball of 4ply silk/mohair yarn in white (B)
One 25g/210m ball of 4ply silk/mohair yarn in grey (C)
One 25g/210m ball of 4ply silk/mohair yarn in black (D)
NOTE: all yarns are used double throughout
Pair each of 3.25mm and 6mm knitting needles
Knitter's sewing needle

TENSION

20 sts and 27 rows to 10cm using 6mm needles
    measured over pattern.

FINISHED SIZE

One size fits all.

ABBREVIATIONS

See page 158.

PATTERN NOTE

The yarn is used double throughout and the yarn
combination will be indicated by letters: for example,
a strand of teal and a strand of white will be AB,
or two strands of teal will be AA.

Front and Back (one piece)

Using yarn AC and 3.25mm needles, cast on 145 sts.

Row 1: Knit.

Rep this row five more times.

Change to AD and 6mm needles.

Row 7: [Knit twice into next stitch] to end. *(290 sts)*

Row 8: Purl.

Row 9: Knit.

Row 10: Purl.

Rep last two rows once more.

Change to AA and 3.25mm needles.

Row 13: [K2tog] to end. *(145 sts)*

Row 14: Knit.

Rep last row four more times.

Change to AB and 6mm needles.

Row 19: [Knit twice into next stitch] to end. *(290 sts)*

Row 20: Purl.

Row 21: Knit.

Row 22: Purl.

Rep last two rows once more.

Change to AC and 3.25mm needles.

Row 25: [K2tog] to end. *(145 sts)*

Row 26: Knit.

Rep last row four more times.

Change to AA and 6mm needles.

Row 31: [Knit twice into next stitch] to end. *(290 sts)*

Row 32: Purl.

Row 33: Knit.

Row 34: Purl.

Rep last two rows once more.

Change to AD and 3.25mm needles.

Row 37: [K2tog] to end. *(145 sts)*

Row 38: Knit.

Rep last row four more times.

Change to AC and 6mm needles.

Row 43: [Knit twice into next stitch] to end. *(290 sts)*

Row 44: Purl.

Row 45: Knit.

Row 46: Purl.

Rep last two rows once more.

Change to AB and 3.25mm needles.

Row 49: [K2tog] to end. *(145 sts)*

Row 50: Knit.

Rep last row four more times.

Change to AD and 6mm needles.

Row 55: [Knit twice into next stitch] to end. *(290 sts)*

Row 56: Purl.

Row 57: Knit.

Row 58: Purl.

Rep last two rows once more.

Change to AA and 3.25mm needles.

Row 61: [K2tog] to end. *(145 sts)*

Row 62: Knit.

Rep last row four more times.

Cast off.

To finish

Darn in all loose ends neatly.

Starting at the cast on edge and finishing at the cast off edge, sew the two edges together to create a tube.

Rivals: complementary colours

Although we have described these colours as rivals, it is simply a way of describing their position in relation to each other on the colour wheel: they are the colours that lie opposite each other. However, rather than being true enemies, when placed side by side they can create some interesting relationships.

They say that opposites attract, but one of the most commonly used partnerships in this section, red and green, has more in common than you might think. Both colours are similar in value and are neither the warmest or coolest colours on the wheel. Consequently, they don't react as strongly with each other as other combinations do and have the effect of making the other one appear brighter (or redder/greener) than when they are placed alongside other colours.

Orange is a very warm colour and so when placed against its colour wheel opposite – blue – it will tend to dominate, even when the blue is in equal proportion. So it may be a good idea to use more blue than orange in a design, or to replace orange in its purest form (an equal mix of red and yellow) with tints, tones and shades, such as peach, beige and caramel.

Perhaps the most striking opposites are yellow and violet. The combination looks cheerful in a bed of pansies, but may be quite overwhelming when worked in equal proportions in a garment. Unlike red and green, this pairing differs greatly in value with yellow being the lightest and warmest colour and purple one of the darkest and coolest. As with blue and orange, one option would be to work with different tints, tones and shades of these two colours. Finding just the right balance between these two can be tricky and it is worth swatching your options before starting on a project. It may be better to work with different shades of purple and simply use yellow to highlight aspects of your design.

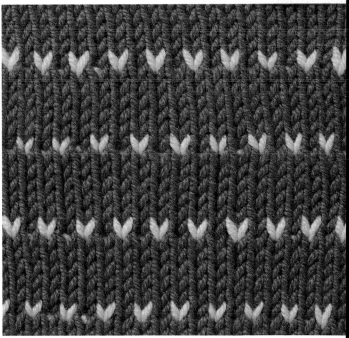

Allies: analogous colours

These partnerships throw up many interesting combinations. The description, 'analogous colours', refers to the relationship between any two (or more), colours that lie next to each other on the colour wheel.

So, if you were looking for colours to go with orange, then red-orange and yellow-orange could be options. An analogous combination of colours may also include the various tints, tones and shades of each of those colours.

One guaranteed way of creating a successful combination is to start by choosing a primary colour and then selecting one of its partners. With blue you could use blue-green or blue-violet; red-orange or red-violet with red; and yellow-orange or yellow-green with yellow. The swatch on the right shows how well blue and blue-green look together. Even when blue-violet is added (far right), the overall effect is still pleasing. This is largely due to the fact that all three colours are mainly blue-based with only small amounts of red present – in blue-violet – and yellow – in blue-green.

However, problems can occur when trying to balance a combination like red with red-violet and red-orange (below right). Unlike the trio of blues, the red-violet and red-orange have larger quantities of yellow and blue in them. This means that there is a high proportion of all three primary colours present, with yellow in red-orange, and blue in red-violet. This creates an uncomfortable scheme with each of the primaries competing with each other.

If you find the design that you are working with needs three similar colours, it is better to start with one of the secondary colours (orange, green, violet), and select from either side of that. This is because two out of these three colours will share some elements of the same primary colour. Here we started with the secondary colour orange and added red-orange and yellow-orange (below far right). The result is pleasing because there are no blue-based colours creating unnecessary tension.

An analogous combination of colours may also include the various tints, tones and shades of these colours, but again care should be taken when selecting from colour combinations that contain elements of all three primary colours.

Rivals doorstop

This two-colour project brings together a pair of rivals whose contrasting relationship creates a dramatic palette. The cool red-violet and its opposite, a warm lime green, aren't the coolest and warmest on the wheel and so even though they are rivals, they aren't so contrasting that the palette doesn't work – in fact, they make a good team!

MATERIALS

Two 50g/125m balls of DK yarn in pink (A)

Two 50g/125m balls of DK yarn in green (B)

Pair of 4mm knitting needles

60cm 4mm circular needle

Pair of 4mm double-pointed needles

Knitter's sewing needle

Four 2cm buttons

Toy stuffing

Dried peas or rice

TENSION

22 sts and 30 rows to 10cm using 4mm needles measured over st st.

FINISHED SIZE

19 x 19 x 19cm.

ABBREVIATIONS

See page 158.

Sides A and C (both alike)

Using yarn A and 4mm knitting needles, cast on 41 sts.

Using the intarsia technique and changing colours as indicated, work rows 1–53 from Chart 1.

Using yarn A.

Row 54: Purl.

Cast off.

Sides B and D (both alike)

Using yarn B and 4mm knitting needles, cast on 41 sts.

Using the intarsia technique and changing colours as indicated, work rows 1–53 from Chart 2.

Using yarn B.

Row 54: Purl.

Cast off.

Top

Sew the four sides into a strip following diagram provided. Then work as follows:

With RS facing and using yarn A and 4mm circular needle, pick up and knit 162 sts across the top edges of the four squares: 41 sts across top of first square, 40 sts across top of second, 40 sts across top of third and 41 sts across top of fourth.

Row 1 (WS): Knit.

Change to yarn B.

Row 2: K1, k2tog, k36 [ssk, k2tog, k36] to last 3 sts, ssk, k1. *(154 sts)*

Row 3: Purl.

Row 4: K1, k2tog, k34 [ssk, k2tog, k34] to last 3 sts, ssk, k1. *(146 sts)*

Row 5: Purl.

Row 6: K1, k2tog, k32 [ssk, k2tog, k32] to last 3 sts, ssk, k1. *(138 sts)*

Row 7: Purl.

Row 8: K1, k2tog, k30 [ssk, k2tog, k30] to last 3 sts, ssk, k1. *(130 sts)*

Row 9: Purl.

Row 10: K1, k2tog, k28 [ssk, k2tog, k28] to last 3 sts, ssk, k1. *(122 sts)*

Row 11: Purl.

Row 12: K1, k2tog, k26 [ssk, k2tog, k26] to last 3 sts, ssk, k1. *(114 sts)*

Row 13: Purl.

Row 14: K1, k2tog, k24 [ssk, k2tog, k24] to last 3 sts, ssk, k1. *(106 sts)*

Row 15: Purl.

Row 16: K1, k2tog, k22 [ssk, k2tog, k22] to last 3 sts, ssk, k1. *(98 sts)*

Row 17: Purl.

Row 18: K1, k2tog, k20 [ssk, k2tog, k20] to last 3 sts, ssk, k1. *(90 sts)*

Row 19: P1, p2togtbl, p18 [p2tog, p2togtbl, p18] to last 3 sts, p2tog, p1. *(82 sts)*

Working decreases as set by last two rows, continue decreasing on every row until 18 sts remain, ending with a WS row.

Thread yarn through remaining 18 stitches and pull tight.

Base

Using yarn A and 4mm knitting needles, cast on 41 sts.

Row 1: Knit.

Row 2: Purl.

Rep last two rows until 56 rows have been worked, ending with a WS row.

Cast off.

Handle

Using yarn A and 4mm double-pointed needles, cast on 5 sts.

Row 1: Knit.

Do not turn knitting, instead slide the stitches to the other end of the double pointed needle ready to be knitted again. The yarn will now be at the left edge of the knitting and so to knit you must pull it tightly across the back of the work and then knit another row. Continue in this way, never turning and always sliding the work to the other end of the double-pointed needle so the right side of the work is always facing you.

Rep row 1 until cord measures 15cm from cast on edge.

Break off yarn, thread through remaining stitches and pull tight.

Fold cord in half to form a loop and stitch the cast on edge to the last row.

To finish

Darn in all loose ends neatly.

Starting at the bottom, sew the remaining side of square A to the remaining side of square D and sew all the way up to the end of the shaping at centre top.

With right side facing, sew the base to the bottom edges of each of the four side squares, leaving one seam open for inserting stuffing.

STUFFING

The doorstop is predominantly filled with toy stuffing, but to achieve the weight that it needs we suggest putting a layer of dried peas or rice at the bottom (in a fabric bag) and then insert the toy stuffing on top of this.

To achieve the studded effect, using the photograph as a guide sew each of the four buttons in place, lacing the thread from side to side through the centre of the doorstop.

Finally, stitch the loop handle in place at the centre top.

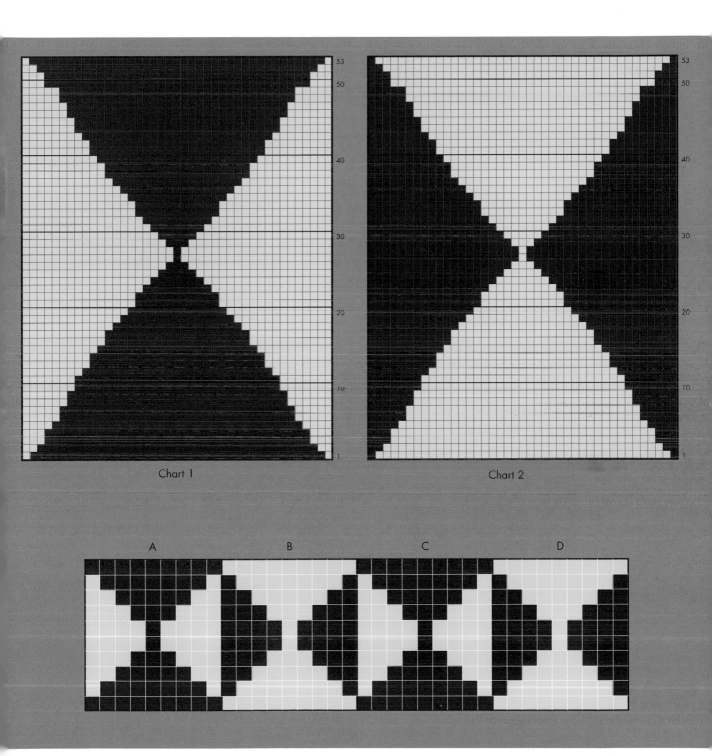

Chart 1

Chart 2

A   B   C   D

3

Proportion and stitchwork

Now that we have explored colour relationships, we must consider the impact that proportion and stitchwork can have on those relationships. This chapter will look at the importance of these two factors by exploring:

— how proportion impacts the balance of a design.

— the ratios of colours within an existing design and how to change them.

— the effect that a chosen colour technique has on proportion.

— what to consider when planning proportion.

— how textured stitches reveal the tints, tones and shades within a single colour.

— how stitchwork can help us to manipulate the use of a colour within a pattern.

— the effects of different yarns.

Ratio of colours to one another

So far we have explored colour relationships and how colours react to each other, which – as we've discovered – is an essential part of creating a successful palette. However, that alone is not enough – we need to consider proportion, too. Proportion is one of the main principles of design and is extremely important when putting colours together: get the proportion of colours and space right and you are well on your way to success.

Stripes

Let's look at stripes first of all, as stripes are a good way of illustrating the importance of proportion. If you want to put together a multi-coloured striped sequence for your own project, it is difficult to know where to start and how much of each colour to use. The swatches shown here explore different possibilities.

We have chosen four colours – a teal blue, a lime green, a burnt orange and a rich brown. The blue and green are a cool combination with the brown and orange warming up the palette.

The first swatch features each of the four colours used just once, each worked in a wide stripe. In the second swatch, the width of the stripes has been halved, and so each colour features more than once. The width of the stripes in the third swatch is halved again.

If you compare these three swatches, you will notice that the interest in the design increases as the stripes become narrower. The narrower the stripe, the more often a colour is used and this gives the eye more to look at.

These are stripes formed using equal amounts of colours, but what happens if we start to vary the width of the stripes?

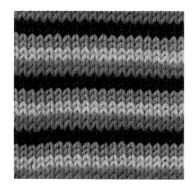

This swatch uses the same four colours, but this time the blue and green dominate (wider stripes), while the brown and orange have been used in smaller amounts (narrower stripes) as supporting colours.

This swatch uses the same stripe pattern, but the orange and brown have swapped places with the blue and green, and what a difference it makes! Varying the width of your stripes, and therefore the proportion of the colours used, has a knock-on effect on your palette. The swatch on the left is a lot cooler than the swatch on the right.

'These two swatches are also an example of asymmetrical balance, which is the term used for a design that uses unequal proportions. The first three swatches, which used equal proportions, are examples of symmetrical balance. Asymmetrical designs are often deemed more interesting, while symmetrical designs can sometimes be termed as visually boring.'

Other colour techniques

What we have learnt so far about proportion in relation to stripes is a big help, but we must also consider designs that are multi-coloured but not necessarily stripes, for example Fair Isle and intarsia designs. We will be exploring these techniques in more detail in Chapter 5 (see pages 106–123) and Chapter 6 (see pages 124–147), but have a look at the swatches below to see how a chosen method of colour work (stripes, Fair Isle, intarsia) can impact on proportion.

 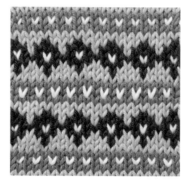 

These different techniques of knitting with colour allow you to place colours in different areas and in different amounts. For example, Fair Isle allows you to place a single stitch of colour, whereas if you are working in stripes the minimum amount of one colour is a row. Intarsia enables you to place blocks of colour and, unlike stripes and Fair Isle, allows you to distribute colours vertically as well.

  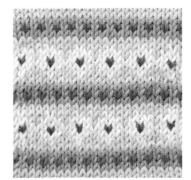

Once you have decided what technique you are going to use, you then need to look at the proportions of colours within that. For example, with Fair Isle, experimenting with the proportions of your chosen colours can dramatically change the appearance of a palette. These three swatches all use the same four colours – teal blue, light blue, lemon yellow and a lime green – but each swatch looks very different due to the change in the proportions of the colours used.

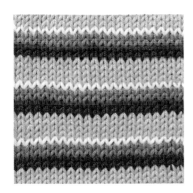  

It's not just the colour work technique that can impact how colours are distributed, the chosen stitch can affect it, too. Reverse stocking stitch and moss stitch allow the change of colour to be viewed on the right side of the knitting, adding an extra dimension. We will be exploring in detail the effect of stitch work on colour later in this chapter (see pages 78–82), but have a look at these swatches to see what these stitches do to proportion. The proportions of colours to one another stays the same, but in the reverse stocking stitch and moss swatches the colours are visually broken up into smaller amounts and appear to feature more often than they do in the stocking stitch swatch.

How many colours to use

When planning a colour palette, you need to decide on how many colours to use within it. If you choose to use just two, the viewer's eye tends to bounce back and forth between them, unsure as to what they should be looking at. For this reason, varying the proportion of the two colours can help a two-colour design.

These two swatches show the same two colours – purple and green – worked in a striped chevron. The swatch on the left uses the two colours in equal proportions, but the swatch on the right uses different proportions – the purple dominates with the green used as an accent. This swatch works well, allowing both of the two colours space to breathe.

However, you might find it easier to create a balance between colour and proportion by using three or more colours. This swatch is the same pattern as the one shown above left, but it has had a hot pink added to it. The introduction of a third colour enhances the design and stops your eye bouncing back and forth between only two colours.

It is also worth noting that hot pink was chosen because it is an ally of purple and this close relationship adds to the interest of the proportion. Even though the chevron stripes are of equal widths (2 rows), the eye tends to read the pink and purple together and the green then takes on the role of an accent colour.

If you want to use three or more colours in your palette, it is a good idea to decide which is your main colour, which colours will be your supporting ones and which your accent. Depending on your total number of colours you could divide them up as follows:

3 colours   a main, a supporting and an accent
4 colours   a main, two supporting and an accent
5 colours   a main, three supporting and an accent

Odd numbers

When you are deciding how often to use a colour within a design, odd numbers are very pleasing to the eye – much more so than even numbers. This is a rule that gardeners often stick to; when planting, they will use odd numbers of plants as opposed to even ones.

On the left are two colours in two vertical strips. The effect is similar to the point made earlier about the eye bouncing back and forth, but If we add a third vertical strip (to make an odd number), one colour automatically becomes dominant. This creates asymmetrical balance and the swatch is altogether more pleasing to the eye. It could also be argued that the use of odd numbers gives a design a beginning, a middle and an end, making it complete.

If you use a colour in a design and then start to be unsure of whether it works, try introducing it again and you will probably find that it does. This is not always the case, but more often than not, using a colour more than once adds to its success and it's definitely worth trying before re-thinking your colours.

Changing the ratio of colours in an existing design

If you want to change the ratio of colours within an existing design (that is to say, change the position of each colour), it is wise to first of all establish what the ratio relationships are within the existing design. How many colours have been used? Which is the main, which is/are the supporting colour/s and which is the accent colour? Once you have established these relationships, it is a lot easier to set about finding successful alternative palettes.

Swatching all the possible combinations is the best way to decide what you personally like or don't like, but the following exploration illustrates what a difference the ratio of colours to each other can have on a palette.

Let's look at the slip stitch panel on the hue family bag (see pages 26–29). Three different shades were used in the panel – a hot pink, a sugar pink and a dusky pink. The sugar pink is the main, the dusky pink is the supporting colour and the hot pink is the accent.

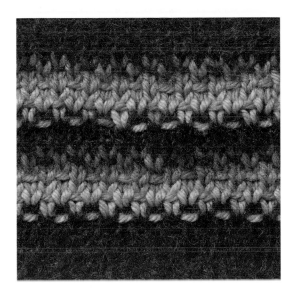

If we swap the main and the accent colour the change is quite dramatic, as what we originally chose as just an accent is now dominating, and vice versa.

If we swap the supporting colour and the accent colour, you will see that the change is less dramatic. This is because the main colour has remained the same and so the overall appearance is very similar to the original.

Yarns types and needles sizes

Proportion can be further altered by using different ply yarns. For example, one stitch of very fine yarn will have little impact, but a stitch of the same colour in a much thicker yarn will have more of a presence. To achieve this effect, consider plying up yarns (using several strands) to achieve greater impact.

Varying needle size can also impact proportion – try knitting a fine yarn on a large needle and the effect will be a diluted version of the stitch had it been knitted on the correct needle size.

However, if we swap all three so that none of the colours are in their original positions, we achieve a look that's quite different to the original.

Stripe hot water bottle cover

A warm palette of coral, red, bronze and gold was chosen to give this winter accessory a cosy feel, and reverse stocking stitch has been used to soften the changes between the colours. Within the stripe sequence itself the bronze dominates, but overall the coral and red dominate, which is further accentuated by the addition of the coral buttons. The back of the design is asymmetrical with the button flap contrasting with the stripe panel, but the front is a nod towards a more symmetrical design.

MATERIALS

One 50g/120m ball of DK yarn in coral (A)
One 50g/113m ball of DK yarn in red (B)
One 50g/113m ball of DK yarn in yellow (C)
One 50g/113m ball of DK yarn in gold (D)
Pair each of 4mm and 3.75mm knitting needles
Two stitch holders
Knitter's sewing needle
Three 18mm buttons

TENSION

22 sts and 30 rows to 10cm using 4mm needles
    measured over rev st st.

FINISHED SIZE

Width: 23cm.
Length to neck: 27cm.

ABBREVIATIONS

See page 158.

Front

Using yarn A and 4mm needles, cast on 37 sts.

Row 1 (RS): Purl.

Row 2: Knit.

Row 3: Inc into first st, purl to last st, inc into last st. *(39 sts)*

Row 4: Inc into first st, knit to last st, inc into last st. *(41 sts)*

Rep last two rows once more. *(45 sts)*

Change to yarn B.

Row 7: Inc into first st, purl to last st, inc into last st. *(47 sts)*

Row 8: Inc into first st, knit to last st, inc into last st. *(49 sts)*

Change to yarn C.

Row 9: Inc into first st, purl to last st, inc into last st. *(51 sts)*

Change to yarn D.

Row 10: Inc into first st, knit to last st, inc into last st. *(53 sts)*

Row 11: Purl.

Row 12: Knit.

Change to yarn B.

Row 13: Purl.

Change to yarn C.

Row 14: Knit.

Rows 1–14 set the stripe pattern. Rep rows 1–14 (without shaping) four more times, ending with a WS row.

Cont in yarn A only.

Row 71: P2tog, purl to last 2 sts, p2tog. *(51 sts)*

Row 72: K2tog, knit to last 2 sts, k2tog. *(49 sts)*

Row 73: P2tog, purl to last 2 sts, p2tog. *(47 sts)*

Row 74: K2tog, knit to last 2 sts, k2tog. *(45 sts)*

Row 75: P2tog, purl to last 2 sts, p2tog. *(43 sts)*

Row 76: Knit.

Row 77: Cast off 3 sts, purl to end. *(40 sts)*

Row 78: Cast off 3 sts, knit to end. *(37 sts)*

Rep last two rows once more. *(31 sts)*

Row 81: Cast off 4 sts, purl to end. *(27 sts)*

Row 82: Cast off 4 sts, knit to end. *(23 sts)*

Leave these 23 sts on a holder.

Lower back

Using yarn A and 4mm needles, cast on 37 sts.

Row 1 (RS): Purl.

Row 2: Knit.

Row 3: Inc into first st, purl to last st, inc into last st. *(39 sts)*

Row 4: Inc into first st, knit to last st, inc into last st. *(41 sts)*

Rep last two rows once more. *(45 sts)*

Change to yarn B.

Row 7: Inc into first st, purl to last st, inc into last st. *(47 sts)*

Row 8: Inc into first st, knit to last st, inc into last st. *(49 sts)*

Change to yarn C.

Row 9: Inc into first st, purl to last st, inc into last st. *(51 sts)*

Change to yarn D.

Row 10: Inc into first st, knit to last st, inc into last st. *(53 sts)*

Row 11: Purl.

Row 12: Knit.

Change to yarn B.

Row 13: Purl.

Change to yarn C.

Row 14: Knit.

Rows 1–14 set the stripe pattern. Rep rows 1–14 (without shaping) twice more and then rows 1–6 again, ending with a WS row.

Change to yarn B and 3.75mm needles.

Row 49: Knit.

Row 50: P4 [k3, p3] to last 7 sts, k3, p4.

Row 51: K4 [p3, k3] to last 7 sts, p3, k4.

Rep last two rows twice more.

Row 56: P4 [k3, p3] to last 7 sts, k3, p4.

Cast off in rib pattern.

Upper back

Using yarn B and 3.75mm needles, cast on 53 sts.

Row 1: K4 [p3, k3] to last 7 sts, p3, k4.

Row 2: P4 [k3, p3] to last 7 sts, k3, p4.

These two rows set the rib pattern.

Row 3: Rib 7 [k2tog, yfwd, rib 16] twice, k2tog, yfwd, rib 8.

Row 4: P4 [k3, p3] to last 7 sts, k3, p4.

Row 5: K4 [p3, k3] to last 7 sts, p3, k4.

Row 6: P4 [k3, p3] to last 7 sts, k3, p4.

Change to yarn A and 4mm needles.

Row 7: Knit.

Row 8: Knit.

Row 9: Purl.

Rep last two rows six more times.

Row 22: Knit.

Row 23: P2tog, purl to last 2 sts, p2tog. *(51 sts)*

Row 24: K2tog, knit to last 2 sts, k2tog. *(49 sts)*

Rep last two rows once more.

Row 27: P2tog, purl to last 2 sts, p2tog. *(43 sts)*

Row 28: Knit.

Row 29: Cast off 3 sts, purl to end. *(40 sts)*

Row 30: Cast off 3 sts, knit to end. *(37 sts)*

Rep last two rows once more. *(31 sts)*

Row 33: Cast off 4 sts, purl to end. *(27 sts)*

Row 34: Cast off 4 sts, knit to end. *(23 sts)*

Leave these 23 sts on a holder.

To finish

Darn in all loose ends neatly.

Sew Front to Upper Back by sewing together the left hand
   sets of cast off stitches.

NECK OF COVER

With RS facing and using yarn B and 3.75mm needles, knit
22 sts from Front holder and then knit last st tog with first st
from Upper Back holder, knit to end. *(45 sts)*

Row 1 (WS): P3 [k3, p3] to end.

Row 2 (RS): K3 [p3, k3] to end.

Rep last 2 rows until neck measures 7.5cm, ending with WS
   facing for next row.

Change to yarn A

Next row: P3 [k3, p3] to end.

Cast off loosely in rib pattern.

Line up Lower Back with Upper Back, ensuring that the ribs
overlap, and sew around all edges, leaving row ends of rib
on Upper Back open.

   Position the three buttons along the rib of the Lower Back
so that they line up with the buttonholes and sew in place.

Stitchwork

Stitchwork and texture often go hand-in-hand with our colour choices. It's hard to think of one without the other. How often have you been attracted to the colour of a ball of yarn or garment on display and reached out to touch it? It is this fusion of colour and texture that also has a part to play in our selection.

We would probably all be happy to agree that textured and cabled stitches look better in pastels, lighter tints and neutrals. It is not often that we see cables worked in very dark colours. Our choice of classic cream in these examples helps to emphasize the interplay between light and dark on the surface of these swatches.

The combination of stitches used in the top left swatch shows how texture can affect the appearance of a colour. The stocking stitch areas tend to reflect the light and appear to have more sheen, while the reverse stocking stitch areas appear to be duller and flatter. The moss stitch areas share both these elements, with light bouncing off the bumps of the purled stitches. The remaining swatches (Blind Button Hole, Bramble and Cable), all create surfaces of different tonal values that help us to see where tints, tones and shades might be used in future colour choices and designs.

'Texture can have more effect on a one-colour project than you might think, so you must always consider it when picking a colour for a project.'

The contrast between light and shade can be further explored by using different stitch patterns with two or more colours.

This breaking up and re-aligning of colours gives an impression of greater harmony than simple stripes might. In each of these swatches we have used neutrals to demonstrate how the stitches work, but the swatches should also give you an idea of how you might use their relative values to help you choose from any one of the colour families.

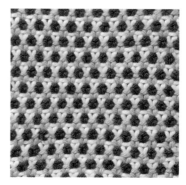

One of the easiest and most effective ways of working with more than one colour is to work a basic slip stitch pattern, a combination of slipped and knitted stitches. In this example you can see how the contrasting colour is held in a mesh of the main colour.

For different effects, simply reverse the colours or introduce more colours through a striped sequence. This stitch would work well across all our colour families.

However, there are some stitch patterns that definitely need a dark, medium and light colour in order to achieve the full effect.

The slip stitch technique can be extended into patterns that outline one or more colours against a chosen background. You will see from the swatch that the overall effect is similar to intarsia, but much easier to work with only one colour being used across a row at any one time.

Wrapping and dropping stitches can work in two very different ways. If you are trying to create a fabric with clearly defined areas, then Shadow Box pattern is a good option. It is a good idea to use three contrasting colours so that the lightest one can frame the other two, while the darkest is used to create the shadow.

If you are looking for a less dense stitch with good drape then a pattern that involves dropping stitches will bring more light into play with the colours that you have chosen. We have used two colours to define the stitch and you will see how one tends to dominate because it covers a larger area. It is worth swatching the reverse colourway so that you can be sure you have not only selected the right stitch pattern, but that the colours are working in the proportions that you want.

 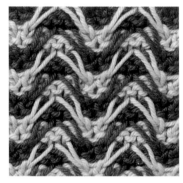 

Twisting or swapping the direction in which the different strands of colour lie can also manipulate the relationship between one or more colours. The twisting in this sample shows how solid, vertical stripes can be made by slipping cable stitches. The embossed effect that this produces will help a chosen colour to literally stand out.

In this example we have chosen a stitch pattern that swaps the direction of dropped stitches, so that one of the two colours is used to decorate the surface of the fabric while the other obscures the stripes of colour that lie behind. Although we have continued to use neutrals, you may like to consider using complementary or warm/cool colours for a highly contrasting effect, or analogous colours for a subtle, even off-beat approach.

Embroiderers often use couching as a way to break up the surface of a fabric and the stitch pattern in this swatch has a similar effect. We have used contrasting colours to demonstrate the full potential of the stitch, but there is no reason why more closely related colours would not work equally well.

Fibre content

When choosing the yarns for this book we selected ranges that offered the broadest palette. It was also important to us that the yarns would work together in order to maximize that range. Each of the yarns from the four ranges has a different fibre content and this in turn affects the colours, depending on the context in which they are used.

 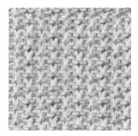  

Double knit cotton is the thickest of the yarns. The 100 per cent pure cotton content means that its smooth surface reflects the light and so appears to have more of a sheen than the pure wool equivalent does. However, it gives clear stitch definition and so works well in our pastel, neutral and cool and mellow colour families.

The pure wool double knit used is slightly finer and gives a smooth, professional finish with a slight sheen that reflects the light. It is less 'crunchy' than its cotton equivalent and works well across all colour families and techniques.

Our third choice is a 50/50 blend of wool and cotton that once again gives great stitch definition. It is spun slightly more tightly than the other yarns and the cotton content means that it will produce a fabric with a slight sheen.

A piece of knitting can be made more light reflective by adding metallic or lurex yarns. This swatch demonstrates how blending and tipping with a metallic yarn can add an extra dimension to colour quality.

Our finest yarn, a combination of 30 per cent silk and 70 per cent kid mohair, offers many possibilities. The sheen of the silk element is best appreciated in neutral and pastel shades, while the fuzziness of the mohair is most evident in 'richer' tones. The overall benefit of the yarn is that it can add lustre to a scheme or design as opposed to sparkle, making it very suitable for blending with other yarns and for tint, tone and shade techniques (see page 52).

Stitchwork cushion

On pages 78–82 we described how use of textured stitches can help to reveal tints, tones and shades within a given colour. Here, the choice of duck-egg blue yarn and a multi-textured stitch pattern combine to produce a fabric that reflects dark, light and mid-tones.

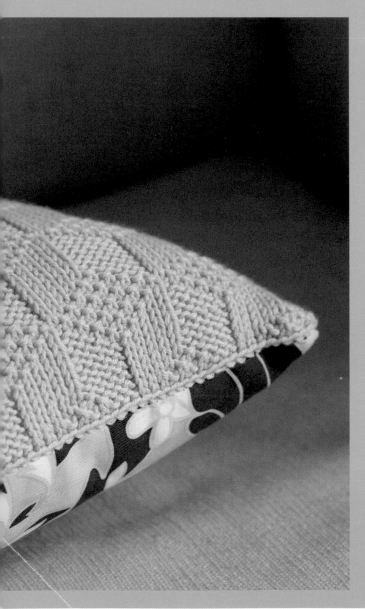

MATERIALS

Two 50g/120m balls of DK yarn in duck-egg blue

Pair of 4mm knitting needles

Knitter's sewing needle

Piece of fabric measuring approx 48 x 38cm

Sewing machine

Sewing thread

Sewing needle

Cushion pad measuring 45 x 35cm

TENSION

20 sts and 30 rows to 10cm using 4mm needles measured over pattern.

FINISHED SIZE

45 x 35cm.

ABBREVIATIONS

See page 158.

Front

Cast on 90 sts.

Row 1: [K1, p1] to end.

Row 2: [P1, k1, p1, k2, p2, k1, p1, k1] to end.

Row 3: [K1, p1, k3, p3, k1, p1] to end.

Row 4: [P1, k4, p4, k1] to end.

Row 5: [K5, p5] to end.

Rows 6–8: As row 5.

Row 9: [K4, p1, k1, p4] to end.

Row 10: [K3, p1, k1, p1, k1, p3] to end.

Row 11: [K2, p1, k1, p1, k1, p1, k1, p2] to end.

Row 12: [K1, p1] to end.

Row 13: [P1, k1] to end.

Row 14: [P2, k1, p1, k1, p1, k1, p1, k2] to end.

Row 15: [P3, k1, p1, k1, p1, k3] to end.

Row 16: [P4, k1, p1, k4] to end.

Row 17: [P5, k5] to end.

Rows 18–20: As row 17.

Row 21: [K1, p4, k4, p1] to end.

Row 22: [P1, k1, p3, k3, p1, k1] to end.

Row 23: [K1, p1, k1, p2, k2, p1, k1, p1] to end.

Row 24: [P1, k1] to end.

Rep rows 1–24 three more times and then rows 1–10 once
    more, ending with a WS row.

Cast off.

To finish

Darn in all loose ends neatly.

Using the knitted cushion Front as a template, cut backing
fabric to size, allowing a 1.5cm seam allowance all the
way around. Right sides together, machine sew the fabric to
the cushion front, leaving one side open for inserting the
cushion pad. Turn right side out. Insert cushion pad and slip
stitch final seam.

4

Colour and decoration

In this chapter we will look at some of the additional strategies available to the knitter when working with colour. Expand your colour knitting horizons by discovering:

- how different-coloured knitted backgrounds affect a single bead colour.

- the effect of different-coloured beads on a single-colour knitted background.

- how knitted flowers and motifs can help to harmonize or accent different aspects of a design.

- an outline of how different embroidery stitches and techniques can support a colour scheme.

- the decorative as well as the functional potential that choice of buttons can bring to your work.

- the interest that cast-ons, borders and frills can add to plain and patterned knitted fabric.

Techniques

A simple, but very effective, technique for knitting beads into a fabric is shown here.

Threading beads onto yarn

Before you start beaded knitting, you need to get the beads onto the yarn.

1 Thread a length of sewing cotton through the eye of a fine sewing needle and tie the two ends together with a secure knot – this will form a loop. Thread the knitting yarn through the loop.

2 Slide a bead over the sewing needle, down the thread and onto the knitting yarn.

Slip stitch beading

There are various beading methods, but this is the simplest and the one we most often use.

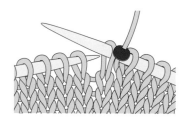 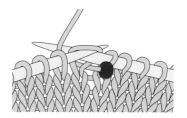

1 Work to where you want to position the bead. Bring the yarn forward between the needle points and slide a bead up the yarn until it sits tight against the front of the work, then slip the next stitch purlwise.

2 Take the yarn back between the needle points and knit the next stitch firmly. You might need to nudge the bead slightly to make sure it stays at the front.

Threading beads on in the right order

If you are working with more than one colour of bead, the beads will need to be threaded onto the yarn in a specific order.

The last bead you thread onto your yarn will be the first one that you knit with, so you will need to thread beads onto your yarn in reverse order. This will involve reading the chart from the top (that is, from the last beaded row), and from left to right on right side rows.

It is a good idea to write out the order of beads as well and then check this against the chart, prior to threading. I often double-check by reading the chart and then counting the beads as they have been threaded onto the yarn, just to make sure that they correspond.

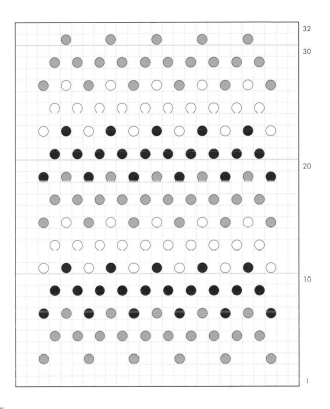

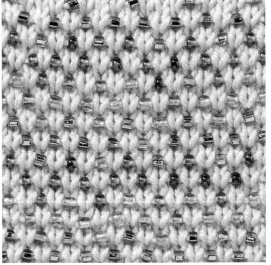

In this swatch we used 63 beads in A (turquoise), 63 beads in B (lime) and 42 beads in C (amethyst) and threaded them onto the yarn in the following order: 16A [1C,1A] 5 times, 11C [1B,1C] 5 times, 11B [1A, 1B] 5 times, 11A [1C, 1A] 5 times, 11C [1B,1C] 5 times, 11B [1A, 1B] 5 times, 16A.

Beading and colour families

The knitting in of beads adds an extra dimension to the fabric of knitted projects. As well as adding texture and making the fabric more tactile, different colouring effects can also be achieved. The possibilities are endless once you start to explore how different colour beads are affected by the background yarn on which they are placed, and vice versa.

  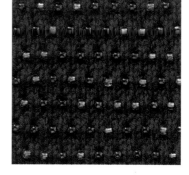

We start by looking at the interplay between beads and yarn in the context of the relationships described in Chapter 2 (see pages 18–63). This first swatch looks at a hue family. Although some of the green beads have more blue and others more yellow in them, the overall effect is harmonized by the mid-green background.

These two swatches show the effect of warm-coloured beads on a cool background and cool-coloured beads on a warm background. In both instances the red dominates, regardless of whether it is the knitted fabric or the bead, because warm colours will always tend to advance.

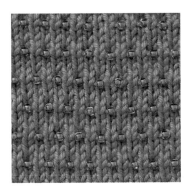  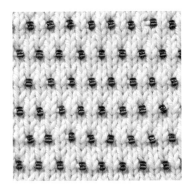

These bright, pastel and neutral swatches show that when yarn and beads are of a similar value, neither will dominate and that the overall effect will be pleasing.

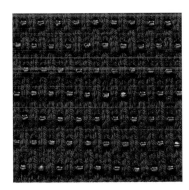  

We also discussed complementary and analogous colour schemes in Chapter 2 (see pages 56–59). These three swatches demonstrate how those relationships could be interpreted in a design by using beads rather than a second yarn.

You will see that we have violet and then red beads on a red-violet background to illustrate analogous relationships and then red-violet on a yellow-green background to illustrate a complementary one.

The small pinpoints of colour that the beads provide offer an alternative to hard stripes and blocks of colour.

Same colour bead on different-coloured backgrounds

We have already said that the overall effect of your beaded knitting will be affected by the choice of bead colour on choice of yarn colour. The following swatches examine how a single bead colour is affected by different-coloured backgrounds.

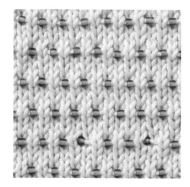  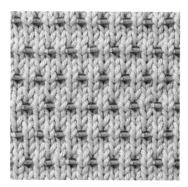

On a pale, neutral background (light grey), the green bead looks bright and vibrant. In stark contrast, the bead is dulled and overpowered by a black background. Used on a browner-based neutral, the green bead once again looks more dominant.

When green beads are set against any colour that has a wholly or strong element of red, it will immediately appear duller. In the swatch on the left, the green bead is undermined by the red yarn. Against the hot pink, it has more impact, but appears a lot bluer than it is in reality. In this set of examples the green bead works most successfully on the violet background. This is because it is a tone of blue-violet and therefore sits not far from green on the colour wheel.

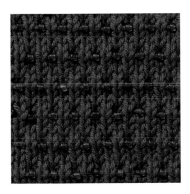

The final set of swatches show how the green beads intensify the background colour. Unlike red, a dark blue background is enhanced by the green beads, while the yellow-green and pale blue backgrounds appear slightly darker than they do on the ball.

Different-coloured beads on same colour background

These swatches examine the effect of different-coloured beads on pieces of knitting that have the same colour background.

In the swatch on the top left you will see that the yarn colour is intensified by the presence of the red beads. This is because pink is derived from red. In the top right and bottom left, the blue bead appears slightly more lilac, while the green bead appears more yellow. Both colours of bead also appear to have drained the pink of some of its vibrancy. Interestingly, when we used a lilac bead of similar value to that of the pink yarn in the bottom right swatch, neither element seem to dominate. This is because both contain equal amounts of red.

'Bear in mind that adding beads to a project can change the way it drapes due to the weight of the beads. Adding a lot of beads can also change the tension of the fabric.'

Adding flowers and motifs

Adding flowers or motifs to your knitting can give you extra
strategies when pulling a colour scheme together. In the same way
that you might accessorize clothes by adding a piece of jewellery
or a scarf, you can do the same with your knitting.

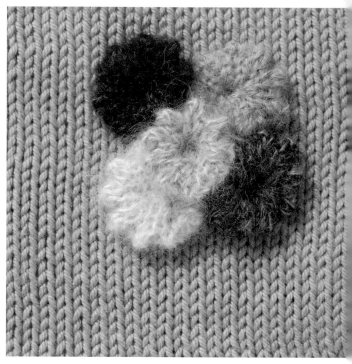

In the swatch on the left you will see how a single colour flower in a mid-pink has
been used to stabilize the striped hue family scheme. In the example on the right,
a single colour background is used as the starting point for exploring a range of
pinks in the flowers.

There will be occasions when a neutral colour scheme is required. If you find that this is starting to look washed out or slightly insipid, then try highlighting a small area with a bright or equally contrasting colour (above left). The motif will then act as an accent, rather than compromising the whole scheme. Similarly, you may find that large areas of a single colour, such as throws and cushions, may benefit from being broken up with a series of motifs (above right).

So far we have looked at how motifs can be used in a supporting role – providing relief or as an accent. This swatch shows how motifs can be used as a purely decorative feature, entitled to a colour scheme in their own right!

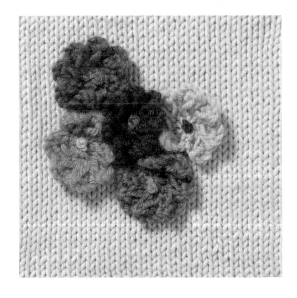

Embroidery

Adding some embroidery to a design is often simple and usually very effective. It is a flexible design feature and can be added to your work at any point. Just like a woven fabric, knitting provides a grid for you to work your stitches on. Try to use the same type of yarn as the knitted fabric as far as possible as this will prevent the fabric from distorting. We have chosen to work the samples using a range of greys, but, like the stitchwork swatches in Chapter 3 (see pages 64–85), these would easily transfer to any palette.

Different stitches can be used in a variety of ways. This first swatch demonstrates some of the simplest embroidery stitches. From top to bottom: running stitch, backstitch, stem stitch, cross stitch and chain stitch. All of these are useful for outlining and joining shapes and motifs.

Swiss darning or duplicate stitch is a great way of adding small areas of detail without going to the effort of joining, stranding or weaving a series of other colours. It can also come in useful when you want to hide a mistake!

This swatch shows Swiss darning worked vertically, horizontally and then as a block. Below that is an example of a lazy daisy, which works equally well as a single motif or in a cluster of one or many colours.

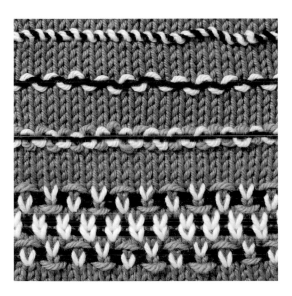

If you want to increase the amount of colour in your embroidered areas, then simply look for stitches that combine more than one strand. Here, basic running stitch and backstitch are embellished by threading different-coloured strands through them. The example at the bottom of the swatch shows how these stitches can be combined with Swiss darning to create more possibilities.

This swatch shows how areas can be outlined and then filled in with embroidery stitches to allow you to place colours and shapes exactly where you want them.

The top left circle is filled in with a continuous chain stitch. This could be worked in one or several colours. The top right circle is outlined with chain stitch and then filled with satin stitch. This works well in small areas with yarns that have a slight sheen. The lower circle is filled randomly with different-coloured French knots. This technique gives you free rein to concentrate as much or as little colour as you want in a specific area.

Buttons

Buttons are usually a very necessary practical part of a garment or an accessory such as a bag. However, there is no reason why they should not also be decorative as well as functional. Historically, buttons were often the most valuable and significant part of an outfit, signifying wealth and status, so it is not surprising that buttons are often used as an integral part of a design.

In the first swatch we have used similar-sized buttons from the same hue family as the yarn. This provides interest, but also a sense of harmony. In the second example, a similar level of interest is created by using strongly contrasting buttons. In the third swatch, the colour of the garment acts as a background or platform for the highly coloured and patterned shell buttons.

'There is nothing wrong with using buttons that are the same colour as the yarn you are knitting with. However, we have looked at some ideas that you may like to consider as a way of adding depth and interest to your work.'

One of the fascinating things about buttons is the range of materials they are made from. Natural elements such as shell, wood and stone can provide a neutral, but very tactile, addition to a plain piece of knitting.

When you simply cannot find the button you are looking for, then you can always make them. Making your own fabric-covered buttons enables you to add small areas of coloured detail. This not only adds interest, but can also act as a link to other garments, accessories and home furnishings. For example, use fabric from curtains to cover buttons that could be used as fastenings on a plain knitted cushion.

Buttons can also be knitted or crocheted. In this swatch, you will see how we have used beaded knitting to cover a button base. This could be complemented by using highly contrasting or even a random selection of coloured beads as part of your scheme. Similarly, Dorset buttons can be worked in a single colour or in three colours to highlight or add relief to plainer sections or areas of knitting.

Edgings

Knitted edgings can impact colour in a number of ways. They can be used to consolidate a palette, to add a burst of colour to a plain project or to provide relief to a multi-coloured palette.

The simplest example of a knitted edging is when you make a feature of the cast on. Here we have explored three different cast-on techniques and what they allow us to do with colour.

This is a simple cable cast on worked in a contrasting colour. A bright lime green for the cast on is in stark contrast to the petrol blue/grey used for the main part of the knitting. Such an edging is a great way of introducing a bright to your project without it overpowering your palette.

A knitted hem gives a professional finish to any project and if worked in a contrasting colour, can be used to provide an occasional flash of colour. Here a bright blue hem has been added to a dark blue swatch. The 'fold over' row has been worked in reverse stocking stitch to create a ridge of colour and if this was worked on a cardigan, a flash of bright blue would be visible when it was worn open. This bright blue could also be used for other aspects of finishing, such as the button band and pocket linings, thus turning what is essentially a one-colour project into a two-colour piece.

A beaded cast on is another way of introducing colour while casting on. Here a complementary pairing of orange and blue has been used. As we have already learned, two complementary colours can sometimes be a little overpowering, but using them here in such different proportions has given a pleasing result.

A knitted edging can be much more than just a cast on. It can be textured, plain, multi-coloured, narrow or deep. These two swatches show a bold palette of five colours – yellow, green, purple, red and teal. The swatch on the left uses a garter stitch chevron edging to introduce four of the colours, with the fifth being used as the main. This is a great way of introducing several colours without the overall look being that of a multi-coloured palette.

The swatch on the right uses the same five colours, but this time all of them have been used in a stripe pattern and just the teal has been used for the edging. Here the one-colour edging consolidates the stripes.

These two swatches have been created from the purple hue family. The swatch on the left shows how a two-colour edging has been used to add interest to a one-colour broken rib. A shade of purple was used for the rib with a tint and tone used for the edging.

The second swatch has been worked from the same palette and this time a Fair Isle design has been enhanced with a knitted frill. The colour of the frill is the colour that has been used least within the Fair Isle patterning, thus giving it more of a presence within the palette.

Beaded needlecase

MATERIALS

Two 50g/113m balls of DK yarn in navy blue

100 green beads (A)

94 pink beads (B)

72 turquoise beads (C)

Pair of 4mm knitting needles

Knitter's sewing needle

Two pieces of lining fabric, each measuring 14 x 39cm

Sewing machine

Sewing thread

Sewing needle

TENSION

22 sts and 30 rows to 10cm using 4mm needles
measured over st st.

FINISHED SIZE

11.5 x 40cm.

ABBREVIATIONS

See page 158.

THREADING THE BEADS

Thread the beads onto one ball of the yarn in the
following order: 4B, 9C, 5B, 1C, 1B, 1C, 1B, 1C, 2B,
1C, 1B, 1C, 1B, 1C, 2B, 1C, 2B, 1C, 2B, 1C, 2B, 1C,
2B, 1C, 1B, 1C, 2B, 1C, 1B, 1C, 2B,1C, 4B, 11A, 4B,
1A, 6C, 1A, 3C, 1A, 4B, 1A, 1B, 1C, 1B, 1C, 1B,
1C, 1B, 1A, 1B, 1C, 1B, 1C, 1B, 1C, 1B, 1A, 1B, 1C,
2B, 1C, 1B, 1A, 1B, 1C, 2B, 1C, 1B, 2A, 1B, 1C, 1B,
1C, 1B, 2A, 1B, 1C, 1B, 1C, 1B, 2A, 1B, 1C, 1B, 2A,
3B, 50A.

Front

Using the beaded yarn, cast on 28 sts.

Row 1: Knit.

Row 2: Purl.

Rep last two rows once more.

Work rows 1–87 from chart.

Next row: Purl.

Next row: Knit.

Rep last two rows twelve more times, ending with a RS row.

** ** Next row:** K3, purl to last 3 sts, k3.

Next row: Knit.

Rep last 2 rows once more.

Next row (WS): Knit, this forms the fold line.

Next row: Knit.

Next row: K3, purl to last 3 sts, k3.

Rep last 2 rows once more.

Cast off.**

Back

Using the yarn without beads, cast on 28 sts.

Row 1: Knit.

Row 2: Purl.

Rep last two rows until 117 rows have been worked ending
    with a RS row.

Work as for Front from ** to **.

To finish

Darn in all loose ends neatly.

    With wrong sides together, sew up sides and base, but
do not stitch past the rows ending K3 (these form part of the
drawstring). Fold over top of each piece at fold line and slip
stitch hem in place, forming a channel. Take care not to close
the sides as these will need to be open for the drawstrings.
Place two pieces of fabric with wrong sides together and
machine sew along sides and base, taking 1.5cm seam
allowances. Place lining inside knitted needlecase,
fold over at the top and hem stitch to knitting at base of
drawstring channel.

DRAWSTRINGS

Cut four lengths of yarn, each 30cm long. Hold two pieces of
yarn together and thread through the front and then the back
channel in the knitting. Tie four strands into a knot close to the
opening. Thread nine beads onto each strand of yarn in the
following sequence, A, B, C three times. Then knot the four
strands together again and snip off ends, leaving 2cm tails.
Repeat, threading second pair of yarns through the back
and then the front channel, so that there is a beaded end on
either side of the needlecase. Pull drawstrings tight to close
the case.

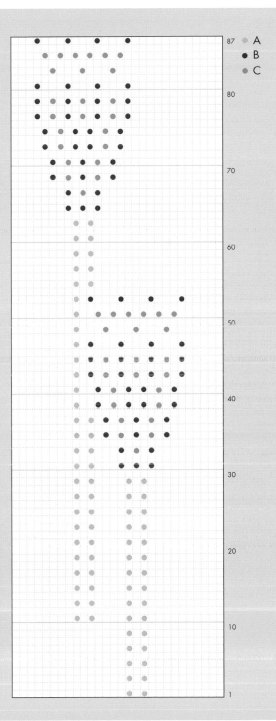

5

Intarsia

Intarsia is an extremely versatile knitting technique, allowing you, the knitter, to knit what you want, in the colour you want, where you want. We will be encouraging you to consider all the possible ways that colour can be used when applying this technique by:

- explaining how the technique is worked.

- showing how to combine single and multi-coloured areas of knitting.

- demonstrating how entrelac can be manipulated to meet your design needs.

- illustrating how bobbles and cables can become not only a textural but also a colourful element of your work.

Techniques

Intarsia knitting is not difficult to master, but if the techniques are unfamiliar to you then we suggest you practise them with scrap yarn before you embark on a project.

Working from a chart

Charts are the easiest and most effective way of showing you how to work a colour pattern in knitting.

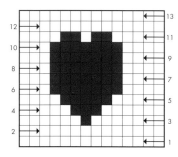

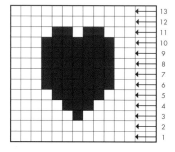

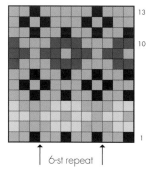

6-st repeat

When working from a chart you start at the bottom and work up. The right-side rows are read from right to left and the wrong-side rows from left to right.

When working a project in the round you must follow a chart in a slightly different way. You still work from the bottom up, but you read every row from right to left, as you are always on the right side of the work.

Not all charts will be provided in full and for a repeating pattern often just a short section – a pattern repeat – will be shown. If this is the case, the chart will show you how you start and finish rows with the repeat in between marked out for you to see.

Difference in shape between charted and knitted motif

When converting motifs into knitted stitches, it is important to remember that knitted stitches are about a third wider than they are tall. Consequently, many knitters prefer to use scaled graph paper that takes these dimensions into account.

Yarn quantity

In order to make up bobbins of different-coloured yarns (see page 110), you need to know roughly how much of each colour is required. A chart is useful for this, too.

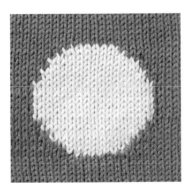
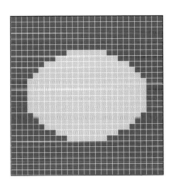

If you prefer to work on ordinary graph paper, remember to compensate for this difference when plotting stitches so that your motif appears 'wider' than it will actually appear when knitted.

Compare the chart with the knitted swatch. In chart form the motif looks like an oval, but in reality knits up as a circle.

Once you have found a motif that you want to reproduce, you will need to draw it onto your chosen graph paper. When you are happy with the shape, make sure that any curves are brought into line with the nearest square on the chart – every aspect of the design has to relate to a stitch.

Be aware that exact replication of a shape is impossible due to the 'V' shape of the knitted stitch. Sometimes a stitch will appear to step just inside or outside the curved and straight lines of your motifs.

A great way of judging how much yarn you need to put into your bobbin is to wrap the yarn around the needle the same number of times as there are stitches for the area you need to knit. Counting the stitches on the chart is the best way of working this out. Add a little extra yarn just to be on the safe side.

Making a bobbin

This is a quick and easy way of making up small bobbins of yarn with which to knit the different-coloured sections of an intarsia design.

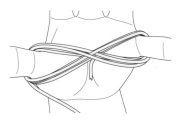 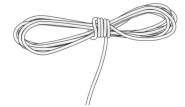 

1 Starting with the working end of the yarn at the centre of your palm, take the working yarn behind your little finger and then across your palm and behind your thumb. Continue in this way, creating a figure of eight.

2 When you have used enough yarn (see page 109), lift the bobbin off your thumb and finger and tie it by wrapping the tail end around the centre. The working end must be left free for use.

3 To start working from the bobbin give the working end a gentle pull, making sure you only pull out a little yarn at a time.

Purchased bobbins

If you prefer, you can wind yarn onto a plastic bobbin rather than making yarn bobbins.

Plastic bobbins can be bought in many haberdashery departments. They are an extremely useful way of organizing your yarns and preventing them from tangling. Plastic bobbins also have the added advantage that the yarn will only slip from the bobbin when the required amount is pulled out by the knitter.

Joining in a colour

With intarsia knitting you will have to join in a new colour of yarn in the middle of a row.

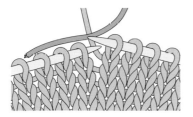
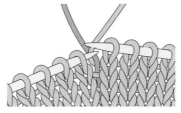
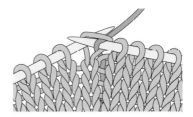

1 Knit to the position of the new colour. With the tail to the left, lay the new colour over the old colour.

2 Take the new colour under and over the old colour.

3 Using the new colour, knit the next stitch. You can give the tail a little pull to tighten the stitch up if needs be. When the knitting is complete, sew the tail into the back of stitches in the same colour yarn.

Eliminating ends

A piece of intarsia knitting can have lots of ends that need to be sewn neatly into the back of the work, which can be a time-consuming job. Where appropriate, use this technique to lessen the number of ends and so shorten the finishing time.

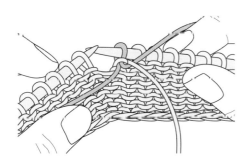
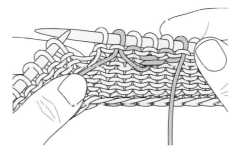

1 Cut a length of yarn long enough to work the entire motif. Find the middle of this by folding it in half, which will create a loop. Use this loop to work the centre stitch of the motif.

2 On the following row, use one end of the yarn to work the right-hand side of the motif and the other to work the left-hand side, making sure you link the background and the motif colour as explained in Changing Colours (pages 112–113).

Changing colours

When you swap from one colour yarn to another, you need to make sure that the yarns are twisted around one another at the back of the work. If they aren't, holes will appear between the different-coloured sections in the knitted fabric.

CHANGING COLOURS IN A STRAIGHT VERTICAL LINE
Sometimes a design will require you to work vertical columns of colour. You achieve this by twisting the yarns to form links between the rows.

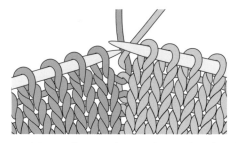

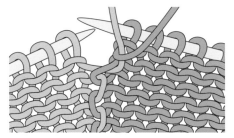

1 When working on a knit row, knit to where the colours need to change. Drop the working yarn and then bring up the new colour from beneath the old one and continue to knit.

2 When working on a purl row, purl to where the colours need to change. Drop the working yarn and then bring up the new colour from beneath the old one, ready to purl the next stitch.

CHANGING COLOURS ON THE DIAGONAL

Although the technique is essentially the same as for changing colours on a straight vertical line, it is important not to over-twist the working yarns.

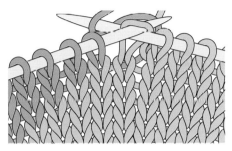

1 When you are extending the diagonal to the right on a knit row, you work to the colour change, drop the working yarn and then bring the new colour up from beneath the old one.

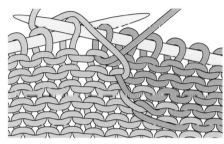

2 When you are extending the diagonal to the left on a purl row, you work to the colour change, drop the working yarn and then bring the new colour up from beneath the old one.

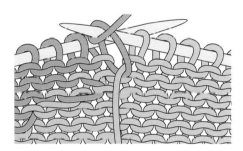

3 When you are reducing the diagonal to the right on a purl row, you work to the colour change, drop the working yarn and then bring the new colour up from beneath the old one.

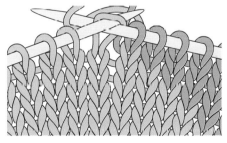

4 When you are reducing the diagonal to the left on a knit row, you work to the colour change, drop the working yarn and then bring the new colour up from beneath the old one.

Shapes and motifs

The intarsia technique can be applied to a variety of knitting situations. It is most commonly used for working large and small motifs and wide, vertical stripes. Some designs use all of these elements to produce complex patterns combining geometric patterning with elaborate motifs. However complex the design, the technique will always produce a single-weight fabric, as opposed to the double weight of Fair Isle.

The following swatches have been worked to demonstrate the various ways of presenting areas of colour in your knitting, as opposed to illustrating specific motifs. This will enable you to make decisions about how much of your design will need to be given over to this technique.

The simplest form of intarsia is created by placing a single, solid-coloured motif within a single, solid-coloured background. The swatch on the left shows two shades of purple, which the eye is able to read simultaneously. Obviously there are numerous ways that this combination could be knitted. The second swatch shows how the motif can be worked in several colours and placed against a solid-coloured background. It is the striped motif that now becomes the focus.

'Sometimes the colours you choose will be dictated by the motif you want to knit. There are many fantastic books full of knitting motifs that you can use to embellish your own knitting projects.'

The swatch on the left is more difficult for the eye to make sense of. The stripes distract the viewer from the central solid-coloured motif. Unless you are working a specific motif that is integral to the original design (for example, floral motifs on a summer cardigan), one of the most successful ways of using intarsia is to work a repeated motif in different colours. The consistent proportional use of colour in the rectangular motif on the right helps to clarify the colour scheme.

Entrelac

The entrelac technique also produces a single-weight fabric. As its name suggests, the fabric appears to be interwoven or interlaced, but this is an optical illusion. Only one colour of yarn is used at a time as the pattern develops. The small sections of colour that are produced are ideal for introducing the entrelac technique and placing little blocks of colour. Different versions of this technique are available, but the one we have used here is based on a multiple of 6 sts.

The left-hand swatch is based on a simple transition from light to dark purple. This would have been obvious if we had used stripes, but the continual off-setting of colours encourages you to consider the overall effect, rather than seeing it section by section. The second swatch is based on the transition from blue to green. Once again, you have to consider the interaction of the colours, rather than a straightforward movement from dark to light and back again.

Pattern

Cast on a multiple of 6 sts.

Foundation row: *P2, turn and k2, turn and p3, turn and k3, turn and p4, turn and k4, turn and p5, turn and k5, turn and p6; rep from * until all sts have been used.

Row 1 (RS): K2, turn and p2, turn and inc in first st, skpo, turn and p3, turn and inc in first st, k1, skpo, turn and p4, turn and inc in first st, k2, skpo, turn and p5, turn and inc in first st, k3, skpo, edge triangle complete; then cont as follows: *pick up and knit 6 sts down side edge of same section of previous row and working across these sts and next 6 sts on LH needle, cont as follows: [turn and p6, turn and k5, skpo] six times; rep from * to last section, pick up and knit 6 sts, turn and p2tog, p4, turn and k5, turn and p2 tog, p3, turn and k4, turn and p2tog, p2, turn and k3, turn and p2tog, p1, turn and k2, turn and p2tog. Fasten off.

Row 2: * With WS facing, pick up and purl 6 sts down side edge of first section of previous row and working across these sts, and next 6 sts on LH needle, cont as follows: [turn and k6, turn and p5, p2tog] six times: rep from *.

Cont to work rows 1–2 until swatch is complete, ending with a row 1.

Finishing row: * With WS facing, pick up and purl 6 sts down side edge of first section of previous row and working across these sts and next 6 sts on LH needle, cont as follows: turn and k6, turn and p2tog, p3, p2tog, turn and k5, turn and p2tog, p2, p2tog, turn and k4, turn and p2tog, p1, p3tog, turn and k3, turn and p2tog, p3tog, turn and k2, turn and p2tog. Fasten off. Rep from * until all closing triangles are completed.

The swatch on the left looks at how an accent can be used within a regular pattern of work. The random use of the yellow-green coloured squares helps to break up the monotony of the neutral colour scheme and provides the eye with a focus.

The final swatch shows how a knitted 'patchwork' can be created. Each section of the fabric is worked at random in a new colour. This constant juxtaposing of colours encourages us to view several different relationships simultaneously. It may not be the most comfortable use of colour, but it allows you to see how flexible this technique can be, leaving it up to the knitter to decide when and where to distribute the colour.

Cables and bobbles

While cables and bobbles are traditionally used to add texture to knitting,
they also lend themselves to the intarsia technique.

Cables are an ideal way of introducing vertical stripes of colour. In the first swatch we see the
simple, but effective, use of a coloured cable on a neutral background. On the right, the use of
a white cable on a coloured background produces a very different effect. Although the cables
require less than half the number of stitches used to work the swatch, they dominate because
they are lighter in value than the background colour. This combined with the texture of the
cables forces the mid-green to play a supporting role.

'There are dozens of cable patterns to choose from, ranging from the
simple rope twists shown here to gloriously intricate designs. Always
work a good-sized swatch to check that your colour ideas work
harmoniously with your chosen cable pattern.'

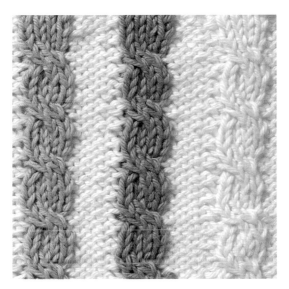 

There is no reason why the uniform structure of cables should impose a rigid colour scheme. The left-hand swatch shows how cables worked in several colours of similar value combine to bring added interest to a neutral background. The use of colour in cables can be extended to combining two colours within one cable. The twisted strands of coloured knitting result in a colourful and decorative piece.

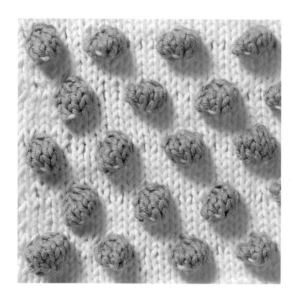 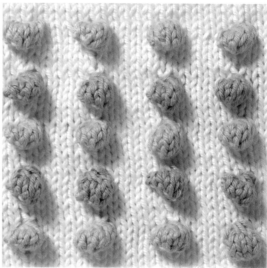

Bobbles are often worked in conjunction with cable patterns. However, when knitted in different colours, they can be used to break up large sections of plain knitting. The first swatch shows how a plain piece of knitting can be transformed by texture and a single colour.

When bobbles are worked in more than one colour, as on the right, they can be used to create patterns and disperse colours. Impact is stronger when two or more colours are worked in regular stripes, rather than when two colours are worked in an off-set pattern. The overall effect is subtler in the third swatch, opposite, and, like the entrelac swatches (pages 116–117), we tend to view the colours as a whole, rather than row by row.

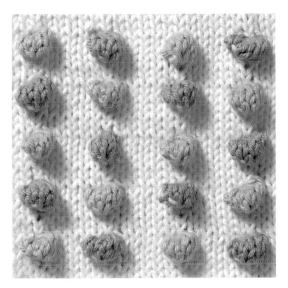

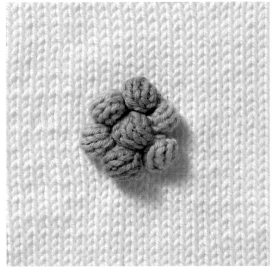

This swatch shows how bobbles can be used to create motifs. Here the bobbles are worked separately and then attached to the knitting – a kind of three-dimensional Swiss darning. The beauty of this technique is that you can add colour and shapes to your exact specification.

'If you work out the pattern carefully, on the row before the bobble you can knit the foundation stitch in the bobble colour to avoid any of the background colour creeping into the bobble.'

Intarsia wall art

Vintage buttons were the inspiration for this piece. A palette of cool blues and greens, warmed up with oranges and accented with chocolate brown, uses nostalgic colours in a contemporary design.

MATERIALS

Three 50g/113m balls of DK yarn in light blue (A)

Two 50g/113m balls of DK yarn in pale lemon (B)

One 50g/113m ball of DK yarn in teal (C)

One 50g/113m ball of DK yarn in yellow (D)

One 50g/113m ball of DK yarn in chocolate brown (E)

One 50g/113m ball of DK yarn in green (F)

One 50g/113m ball of DK yarn in bronze (G)

One 50g/113m ball of DK yarn in orange (H)

Pair of 4mm knitting needles

Knitter's sewing needle

Plain canvas 40cm high x 50cm wide

TENSION

22 sts and 30 rows to 10cm using 4mm needles measured over st st.

Make sure that your tension is accurate as this will determine whether the knitting fits the canvas or not. The work needs to be a snug fit to the canvas and so consider using 3.75mm needles if your tension is borderline.

FINISHED SIZE

40cm high x 50cm wide.

ABBREVIATIONS

See page 158.

Wall art

Using yarn A, cast on 108 sts.

Row 1: Knit.

Row 2: Purl.

Rep last two rows three more times.

Row 9: Cast on 6 sts, knit to end.

Row 10: Cast on 6 sts, purl to end. *(120 sts)*

Row 11: Knit.

Row 12: Purl.

Rep last two rows twenty more times, ending with a WS row.

Using the intarsia technique and changing colours as indicated, work rows 1–54 from chart as follows: (You may find it easier to Swiss darn the single stitch edgings.)

Row 1: K5A, knit 110 sts from chart, k5A.

Row 2: P5A, purl 110 sts from chart, p5A.

Rep last 2 rows twenty-six more times.

Continue in yarn A.

Next row: Knit.

Next row: Purl.

Rep last two rows eleven more times, ending with a WS row.

Next row: Cast off 6 sts, knit to end.

Next row: Cast off 6 sts, purl to end. *(108 sts)*

Next row: Knit.

Next row: Purl.

Rep last two rows three more times.

Cast off.

To finish

Darn in all loose ends neatly.

There is a 2.5cm allowance for a hem all the way around the piece of work. The shaping at each corner allows you to use this hem to create mitred corners as follows:

BOTTOM TWO CORNERS

Sew the edge of the 6 cast on stitches to the side edges of the first eight rows.

TOP TWO CORNERS

Sew the edge of the 6 cast off stitches to the side edges of the last eight rows.

The work should now fit comfortably over the canvas. Turn the canvas over and with the work slightly stretched (check on the front that everything is lining up correctly), complete the back as follows:

Using yarn A and a knitter's sewing needle, lace the two side edges together working back and forth and checking that everything remains lined up correctly on the front. You will have long lengths of yarn stretched across the back of the canvas. Once you have secured the side edges, do the same in the other direction by lacing together the cast on and cast off edges.

Lacing the work onto the canvas in this way allows you to make necessary adjustments by pulling tighter or easing a bit looser according to how the work is lining up on the front of the canvas.

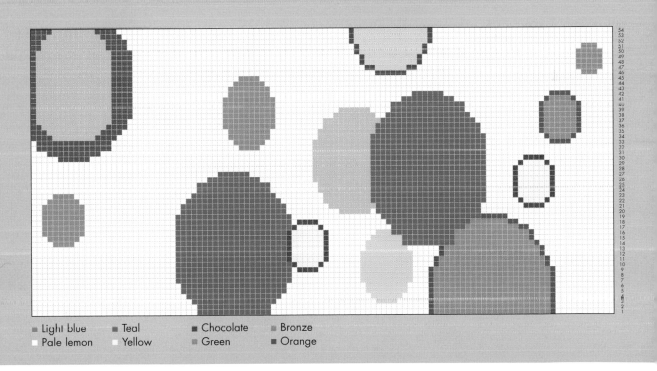

- ■ Light blue
- □ Pale lemon
- ■ Teal
- □ Yellow
- ■ Chocolate
- ■ Green
- ■ Bronze
- ■ Orange

6

Fair Isle

Fair Isle knitting demands two or more colours and so instantly requires you to make colour decisions. This chapter will explore the traditions of the technique through to contemporary reinterpretations of it and will include:

– classic and contemporary aspects of Fair Isle knitting.

– the importance of value within Fair Isle.

– tips on how to re-colour an existing Fair Isle palette.

– tips on how to design a Fair Isle colour palette from scratch.

Techniques

There are various ways of holding the yarns when knitting Fair Isle, and we are always being asked to show people how to work with one yarn in each hand, the fastest Fair Isle technique. So here it is!

Joining in a new colour

To ensure that you have double thickness fabric for the entire row, you must always try and join in a new colour at the beginning of the row (see page 20) and carry it all the way to the end. However, if you must join mid-row, this is how to do it.

ON A KNIT ROW

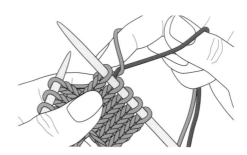

1 Knit to the position of the new colour. Lay the new yarn over the old yarn and twist them together, holding the tail of the new yarn in place on the back with your left index finger.

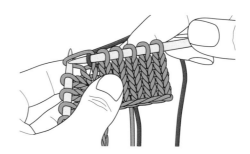

2 Knit the next stitch with the new colour.

ON A PURL ROW

1 Purl to the position of the new colour. Lay the new yarn over the old yarn and twist them together, holding the tail of the new yarn in place on the back with your left thumb.

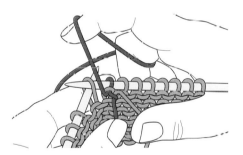

2 Purl the next stitch with the new colour.

Holding yarn in both hands

This technique will almost certainly take a bit of practice to master, but once you can hold the yarns in this way your Fair Isle knitting will really speed up.

ON A KNIT ROW

1 Hold the dominant yarn in your right hand as normal and lay the contrast yarn over the index finger of your left hand.

2 When using the dominant yarn, knit the required number of stitches in the usual way.

3 When using the contrast yarn, 'pick' the yarn off your left index finger with the right-hand needle, going over the yarn.

4 Bring the yarn through the stitch.

5 As you finish the stitch, keep the contrast yarn over your left index finger.

ON A PURL ROW

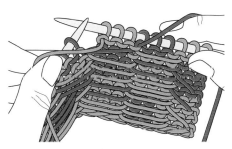

1 Hold the dominant yarn in your right hand as normal and hold the contrast yarn in your left hand, using your thumb.

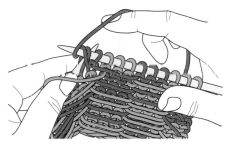

2 When using the dominant yarn, purl the required number of stitches in the usual way, while keeping the contrast yarn over your left thumb.

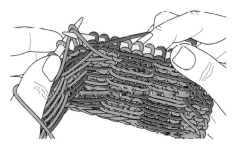

3 When using the contrast yarn, pick up the yarn by placing the right needle under it and lift it up to work the stitch.

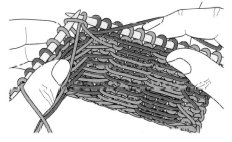

4 Bring the yarn through the stitch, keeping the contrast yarn in your left hand.

Stranding

This is how to strand the yarns across the back of the knitting while working with one yarn in each hand.

ON A KNIT ROW

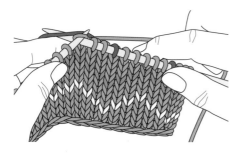

1 Using the two-handed method as previously described and ensuring that the yarn you want to strand is in your left hand, work up to the stitch that you want to strand on. Place the right-hand needle under the contrast yarn on your left index finger.

2 Knit the stitch using the dominant yarn.

3 As you complete the stitch, lift your left index finger slightly to ensure that the contrast yarn doesn't come through the stitch, too.

4 Knit the next stitch, which locks the stranding.

ON A PURL ROW

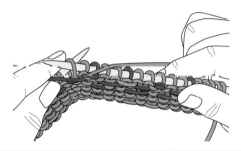

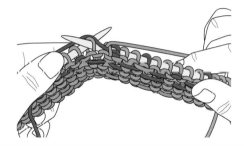

1 Using the two-handed method as previously described and ensuring that the yarn you want to strand is in your left hand, work up to the stitch that you want to strand on.

2 Place the right needle under the contrast yarn that you're holding with your left thumb.

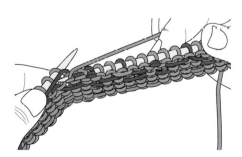

3 Purl the stitch with the dominant yarn, making sure the contrast yarn doesn't come through the stitch, too. Purl the next stitch to lock the stranding.

Traditional Fair Isle

Though its origins lie on the tiny Shetland island of Fair Isle off the coast
of Scotland, this style of colour knitting is now known across the world.
There are some elements that characterize classic Fair Isle designs.

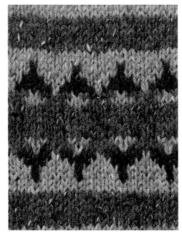

Part of the appeal of traditional Fair Isle
patterns is the subtle use of colour. The
original colours of the Shetland yarns
used by the islanders were the natural
whites, greys and browns produced by
local sheep breeds.

These were combined with colours
made by plant dyes: madder and
indigo were used to produce red and
blue, while lichens gave them green,
brown, orange and purple.

The tweed of the Shetland yarns
gave the colour changes a softness that
made the colours appear to blend into
each other. It wasn't just the yarn alone
that created this lovely 'blend', a great
deal of thought and planning of the
colours used lies behind each
traditional design.

There are three main elements that are
common throughout most traditional
Fair Isles. The first is that the maximum
number of colours used within any one
row is only two – both colours are
carried across the row creating a
double-thickness, warm fabric. The fact
that only two colours have been used
per row might seem surprising when
we admire the complexity of a Fair Isle
design, but it is the skill used in the
planning of the design that makes it
appear more complex.

The second element is the careful selection of colours. The designer will choose two different groups of colours and one will be used for the background and the other for the patterning. The colours within each group will be closely related and sit well with each other, and there will be an element of contrast between the two groups so that the patterning stands out.

The swatch on the right shows how a range of blues has been selected for the background and a range of reds for the patterning. You will also notice that there are different tints, tones and shades within each group and these have been arranged in a certain way, which is the third common feature of traditional Fair Isle design. The background group (blues) starts with the tint at the outer edge of the pattern, then the tone and the shade at the centre. The pattern group (reds) works the opposite way – the shade is at the outer edge working towards the tint in the centre. The chart of the design clearly shows how this has been planned.

These are the common features of traditional Fair Isle designs but you will find many other variations, too. For example, the 'group' of colours doesn't have to be from the same hue family, but will always work best when they have been selected in such a way that they flow nicely into each other. Sometimes the background might be a solid colour rather than a group of colours.

It was not until the 1920s, when chemical dyes became available, that stronger colours started to appear. During the 1940s, the need to 'make do and mend', meant that Fair Isle knitting was a useful way to recycle old garments and so traditional colour schemes were often interpreted in whatever was available.

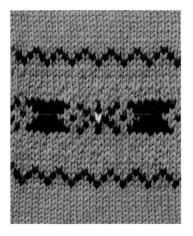

The swatch on the left shows these stronger colours worked against a grey background, which was quite typical. The swatch on the right shows a slightly bolder use of colour that is reminiscent of a 1970s Fair Isle, but the blending of colours associated with traditional Fair Isle is still evident.

Reinterpreting Fair Isle

During the late 1980s and early 1990s, 'Fair Isle' started to be used as a term to describe any type of stranded colour work, regardless of colour scheme or pattern arrangement. Having learned what we have about traditional Fair Isle design (and we have only scratched the surface), it is only right to acknowledge that Fair Isle and stranded knitting aren't really the same thing and instead the name has been adopted for a modern reinterpretation of the original technique.

Colour

The most significant point of difference between traditional and modern Fair Isle-style patterns is the use of colour.

The huge range of colours available to us allows us to put a modern twist on traditional design through the use of colour alone. The swatch shown here is the same design as shown in the brown and beige tweeds earlier (see page 132) – how different it looks when re-worked in a bright palette!

Yarn

Not only do we have vast colour ranges to choose from, we also have extensive yarn types to select from, too.

Rather than producing a piece of Fair Isle from one yarn type, we often see a variety of different-textured yarns used together in one piece. This swatch uses two different-coloured tweeds for the background and the patterning has been worked in a smoother yarn. This contrast in textures adds another dimension to the design, giving the pattern motifs clarity against the fuzziness of the tweed.

Stitch

When stranding colours across the back of the work, the patterning is best displayed on the right side of stocking stitch, but stocking stitch doesn't have to be used for the whole piece.

Framing Fair Isle strips with textured stitches is a great way to add extra interest. Here, wide moss stitch strips have been used to break up the Fair Isle patterning. You could take this further on a project by using moss stitch for other features, such as cuffs or the top band of a bag.

For a really modern re-working of a traditional technique, consider using the reverse of the work. The strands of yarn that are carried across the row can be quite effective as a feature on the right side. However, this works best with a very simple pattern (any complicated pattern is lost), as it's just the stranding that is the focus. It also requires you to make sure you are consistent with your stranding – we always try to make sure the back looks as neat as the front but in this case it would be crucial!

This swatch uses the reverse of a simple 2x2 check as the front. Such a fabric would make a great bag or cushion.

Simplicity

Some knitters are put off working Fair Isle patterns because they think that they are complicated. However, they can be very simple designs.

Just single stitches of colour worked on a different-colour background is about as simple as the Fair Isle technique can get. The swatch shown here has combined this idea with stripes.

Colours have been used to full affect by using pairs of complementary colours – with the exception of the teal/navy analogous relationship, which has been added to provide a little relief.

Another simple yet effective approach to Fair Isle is to use just two colours – one for the background and one for the patterning. The swatch on the left uses a tint and shade of teal – the tint is the background with the shade of teal providing the patterning. As these two colours are from the same hue family the overall effect is quite calming.

The swatch on the right shows another use for just two colours – a simple 2x2 check. Again, it has been knitted using a tint and a shade of the same colour (a raspberry pink) and the contrast between these values shows off the check to full effect.

However, if you wanted to make a bolder statement you could consider varying the relationship between the two colours in either swatch, which would create quite different end results.

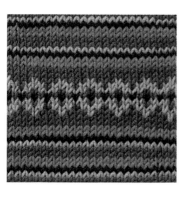

If you want to achieve an all-over multi-coloured design, but perhaps don't want to use the Fair Isle technique throughout, consider combining it with stripes. Fair Isle and stripes make a great pairing, allowing you to echo the use of colours within the two areas while using the stripes to frame the patterning.

Repetition of a motif

We tend to think of intarsia knitting when we think of knitted motifs, but small motifs can be worked across a row using the Fair Isle technique.

Fair Isle and decoration

A great way of putting a fresh twist on this traditional technique is to substitute one of the colours in your Fair Isle pattern with a bead.

The way Fair Isle works right across a row allows us to slot in small motifs instead of the more regular patterning that we usually associate with the technique. The swatch here shows the repetition of a small rosebud design separated by a stripe of alternate single stitches of two colours.

The two swatches above show the same design, but the swatch on the right uses a bright teal bead instead of the teal yarn used in the left-hand swatch. Not only does this allow us to replace the colour, but we've added an extra dimension by choosing a shiny bead. A matt bead would be different again.

The importance of value in Fair Isle

As we have discovered, Fair Isle designs are constructed out of two or more colours. The most successful Fair Isle colour combinations use colours that range in value from near the beginning of the value scale – light – towards the end of the value scale – dark. The following exercise examines the importance of value in Fair Isle and how the proportion of values used can dramatically change the appearance of a Fair Isle design.

We have chosen five colours – purple, magenta pink, lime green, teal and pale teal. Before we decide on these colours as a definite palette, we need to check that they vary enough in value; ideally we need a dark, a light and some mid-tones. It can be quite tricky to do this by eye – not necessarily for the dark and light as these are quite easy to spot, but the mid-tones can be harder to assess. The black and white version of the colour wheel at the beginning of the book will be useful here, but an accurate way of reading the value of your chosen yarns is to simply take a black and white photocopy of them.

Above left you can see our five colours and below, a black and white copy of them. This allows us to see our colours in shades of grey so that we can check that we have enough variance in the values. The purple is the darkest, the pale teal the lightest and the magenta, lime green and teal are the mid-tones. This is a good balance of values.

The proportion in which we choose to use these different values will have an effect on the overall appearance of the end design.

Here we have chosen the two teals to be the background and the purple, magenta and lime green have been used for the patterning. Compare the knitted swatch to the black and white chart to see how the values have been distributed throughout the design.

   If we move the same five colours around within the same design – therefore changing the proportion of the values – what happens?

This variation uses the purple (darkest value) as the main background, but to stop the overall appearance becoming too dark, the lightest value (the pale teal) has been used in a more prominent position.

 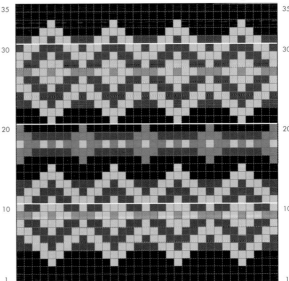

The second alternative uses lime as the main background, which is a mid-tone like the teal of the original swatch, and the magenta has been used in place of the purple, both of which are dark (the purple is the darkest with the magenta sitting at the darker end of the mid-tones). Substituting a colour with one of a similar value doesn't dramatically change the overall lightness or darkness of the palette.

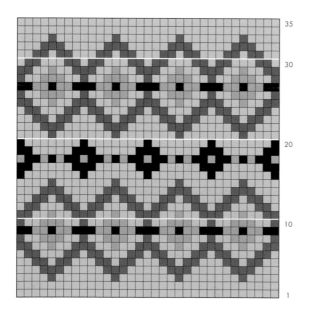

'All four of these Fair Isle swatches are knitted to the same design, although you wouldn't immediately realize that from looking at them as different colours make different parts of the pattern more prominent.'

This third and last version illustrates another point. The lime and the magenta are very similar in value (both mid-tones) and the lime has been used to frame the patterning and sits on a background of magenta. Because they are so close in value, they seem to blend into each other on the black and white chart, and when you look at the knitted swatch this causes it to appear to lack definition between the patterning and the background. This doesn't have to be a negative as it could be the effect that you are striving to achieve.

Changing the proportions of the values has indeed changed the overall appearance of the original design (remembering that all the swatches are exactly the same design, using exactly the same five colours). All were successful in their own right, which illustrates the importance of having a good selection of values (light through to dark) in your chosen palette. You must then decide how light or dark you want the overall appearance to be and then you can distribute the values accordingly.

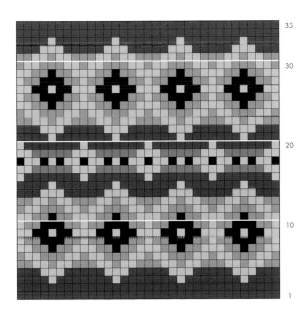

Tips on how to re-colour a Fair Isle palette

Sometimes you might want to re-colour an existing Fair Isle design. It might be because the colours chosen by the designer don't suit you or perhaps the colours used are not available anymore. One way to go about this is to first of all establish the relationships present in the existing design. Once you have identified these, you can then set about finding replacements.

Establishing the existing relationships

Spend some time analyzing the existing palette to determine how it is composed.

Let's look at our original swatch from the value exercise. The relationships between the five colours are as follows:

Magenta and lime are complementary colours.
Magenta and purple are analogous colours.
Magenta and purple and teal and pale teal are cool colours.
Lime green is a warm colour.

We also know that they vary nicely in value: running from darkest to lightest they are purple, magenta, teal, lime and pale teal.

To summarize this existing palette, contrast is provided by the use of two complementary colours, which has been balanced by the use of one of their analogous colours. A good balance between warm and cool colours is for warm to be used slightly less than cool (this is because warm colours are lighter in value and so can dominate – a little goes a long way), and this has been used to full effect here.

Finding colours with similar relationships

Establishing the existing relationships, which we know work well, is a great basis for building a new palette on.

After studying the wheel, we have chosen five colours with similar relationships to those in the existing swatch: dark red-orange, dark olive, sage green, turquoise and lemon.

Dark red-orange and turquoise are complementary colours.
Turquoise and dark olive are analogous colours.
Sage green and dark olive and turquoise are cool colours.
Lemon and dark red-orange are warm colours.

Taking a black and white copy of the palette allows us to check the values and you can see here that the value relationships are similar to the original palette.

To summarize, we have selected colours with similar relationships and we have a similar balance between warm and cool colours.

Putting the colours into the design

All that is now left to do is to decide which colours will go where.

By comparing the black and white values of the original palette and your new palette, you can establish which colours are each other's counterparts. In this case it is as follows.

Purple = dark olive
Magenta = dark red-orange
Teal = sage green
Lime = turquoise
Pale teal = lemon

Replace the original colour with its new counterpart and your new palette is complete.

Tips for creating a Fair Isle palette from scratch

To create a Fair Isle palette from scratch we will, of course, need to draw on the knowledge we have gained so far about colour, value and proportion. But in addition to this, a useful way of forming ideas about a palette is to work from a piece of inspiration.

The piece of inspiration here was a page in one of our sketchbooks, which was made up of lots of things in lovely soft pastel colours. The danger with working in a palette of solely pastels is that it can become a little washed out and so in order to get the balance of values right a neutral has been added – a dark grey – to create some contrast. A quick check using a black and white copy of the chosen yarns confirms that there is enough variance in the values.

We'll use the design from the value exercise again, but this time replacing the colours on the chart with symbols, as this is what you would be faced with if you were working out a colour palette from an existing black and white chart.

Symbols only before colour scheme decided

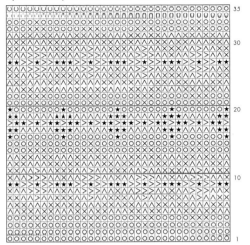

Chart with background colour

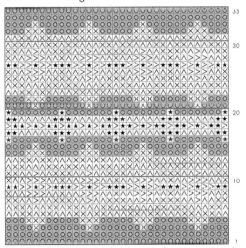

Chart with background colour and patterning colour

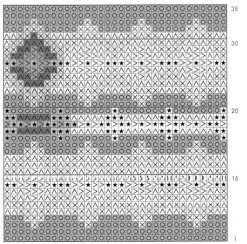

A neutral dark grey has been chosen to act as an antidote to the pastel palette. This will be used only as a background for the pastels to sit on.

Deciding which pastel goes where within the patterning needs a bit more thought. The patterning has two distinct areas – the wide band of diamonds within diamonds and a narrower diamond band.

Let's look at the wide band first, which is the main feature of this Fair Isle. Within the four pastels there is a dark, a mid and two light colours and so to create maximum impact we will place them in such a way that one of the lights separates the mid and dark. This ensures that maximum contrast between the values is achieved.

The narrower diamond band is a secondary feature of the design and so we will choose similar values for this in order to reduce contrast. This ensures that while it is a valuable part of the design, it is also a place for the eye to rest in between the high visual impact of the wider bands.

The final result shows how the introduction of a neutral has given strength to the palette without detracting from the delicateness of the pastels.

As you can see from this exercise, taking time to consider values and colour relationships and how you can use these to produce the effect you want, is the key to creating a successful Fair Isle palette. Don't be afraid to swatch ideas or sketch out charts with coloured pens to find out what you like. Once you've decided on your colours you might then want to move them around to see what proportions are most pleasing to you. Creating a Fair Isle palette can be an exciting and satisfying process that should be enjoyed!

Fair Isle mitts

For this pair of mitts we decided to use fashionable colours such as lime and magenta as a starting point. Interestingly these lie opposite each other on the colour wheel, so we added the complementary shades of a dark teal and lilac. And finally we have included a smart navy and light blue/grey to offset the brighter colours. The result is fresh and modern with a nostalgic twist.

MATERIALS

One 50g/113m ball of DK yarn in navy blue (A)
One 50g/113m ball of DK yarn in light blue (B)
One 50g/85m ball of DK yarn in pink (C)
One 50g/125m ball of DK yarn in green (D)
One 50g/125m ball of DK yarn in teal (E)
One 50g/125m ball of DK yarn in purple (F)
Pair of 4mm knitting needles
Knitter's sewing needle

TENSION

22 sts and 30 rows to 10cm using 4mm needles
    measured over st st.

FINISHED SIZE

One size to fit average-sized adult hand.

ABBREVIATIONS

See page 158.

Mitt (make 2)

Using yarn A, cast on 46 sts.

Join in yarn B.

Row 1: K2 [p2, k2] to end.

Row 2: P2 [k2, p2] to end.

Rep last two rows three more times, ending with a WS row.

Join in yarn C.

Row 9: K2C [p2B, k2C] to end.

Row 10: P2C [k2B, p2C] to end.

Break off yarn C.

Row 11: K2 [p2, k2] to end.

Row 12: P2 [k2, p2] to end.

Join in yarn D.

Row 13: K2B [p2D, k2B] to end.

Row 14: P2B [k2D, p2B] to end.

Break off yarn D.

Row 15: K2 [p2, k2] to end.

Row 16: P2 [k2, p2] to end.

Join in yarn C.

Row 17: K2C [p2B, k2C] to end.

Row 18: P2C [k2B, p2C] to end.

Break off yarn C.

Row 19: K2 [p2, k2] to end.

Row 20: P2 [k2, p2] to end.

Rep last two rows once more, ending with a WS row.

Row 23: Knit.

Row 24: Purl.

Change to yarn A.

Row 25: Knit to end, inc 1 st in centre. (47 sts)

Row 26: Knit.

Using the Fair Isle technique and joining in and breaking off colours as required, work the next sixteen rows from the chart.

Change to yarn A.

Row 43: Knit.

Row 44: Knit.

Change to yarn B.

Row 45: Knit.

Break off yarn B and join in yarns C and F.

Row 46: P1C [p1F, p1C] to end.

Row 47: K1C [k1F, k1C] to end.

Break off yarn C and using yarn F only.

Row 48: Purl.

Change to yarn E.

Row 49: Purl.

Row 50: Knit.

Change to yarn D.

Row 51: Purl.

Row 52: Knit.

Join in yarn B.

Row 53: P1B [p1D, p1B] to end.

Change to yarn A.

Row 54: Knit, this forms the fold line.

Row 55: Knit.

Row 56: Purl.

Rep last two rows once more, ending with a WS row.

Cast off.

To finish

Darn in all loose ends neatly.

THUMBHOLE

With right side facing and on the right hand edge of mitt, pick up and knit 12 sts using yarn A, starting at row 26 and finishing at row 40.

Cast off loosely.

Repeat to match on the left-hand edge of mitt.

Fold hem along fold line (row 54) to inside the mitt and slip stitch in place. Fold mitt in half and sew side seam by working from cast on edge to the start of thumbhole and then from top of thumbhole to top of mitt.

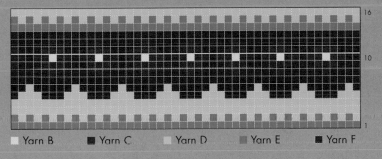

| ☐ Yarn B | ■ Yarn C | ☐ Yarn D | ■ Yarn E | ■ Yarn F |

7

Creativity

This chapter is all about pulling together and applying some of the theories and ideas that we have explored throughout the rest of the book. Ultimately, how you choose to use colour in your work will come from your own individual responses and design criteria. It would not be appropriate to advocate a set of rules that you should rigidly stick to, but we do hope that the following pages will help you to:

–   find ways of using a piece of inspiration to inform your colour choices and selection of materials.

–   organize your thoughts and responses through mood boards and swatches.

–   test your ideas by considering different colour relationships, value, proportion and stitchwork.

–   and finally, to take a risk – it just might work!

Inspiration cushion

Sources of inspiration are many and various, but we have chosen to return to the concept of the hue family as the starting point for our final project. Five different reds that represent a range of values work together to achieve a successful Fair Isle palette. Three bands of Fair Isle framed by four moss stitch bands form the main panel of the cushion. This panel sits next to a simple stocking stitch panel and a moss stitch button band separates the two. In a continuation of the hue family theme, seven different buttons have been used – each is a different shape or size and a varying red.

A cushion is an ideal way of testing out your ideas and over the next few pages you will also discover how we used other sources of inspiration to re-colour this project.

MATERIALS

Two 50g/113m balls of DK yarn in rich red (A)

One 50g/120m ball of DK yarn in coral (B)

One 25g/210m ball of silk/mohair yarn in wine used double (C)

One 50g/115m ball of DK yarn in tomato red (D)

One 50g/115m ball of DK yarn in burgundy (E)

Pair of 4mm knitting needles

Knitter's sewing needle

Piece of fabric measuring approximately 43 x 43cm

Sewing machine

Sewing thread

Sewing needle

Seven buttons of varying sizes, 15–20mm

Cushion pad measuring 40 x 40cm

TENSION

22 sts and 30 rows to 10cm using 4mm needles measured over pattern.

FINISHED SIZE

40 x 40cm.

ABBREVIATIONS

See page 158.

Front Fair Isle panel

Using yarn A, cast on 61 sts.

Row 1: K1 [p1, k1] to end.

This row forms moss stitch.

Rep row 1 twice more.

Change to yarn C.

Rows 4–5: As row 1.

Change to yarn A.

Rows 6–9: As row 1.

Change to yarn C.

Rows 10–11: As row 1.

Change to yarn A.

Rows 12–15: As row 1.

☐ Yarn B   ■ Yarn C   ■ Yarn D

Row 16: Purl

Work rows 17–33 from chart, changing colours as indicated. Change to yarn A.

Row 34: Purl

Rep rows 1–34 twice more and then rows 1–15 once more.

Next row: K1 [p1, k1] to end.

Cast off in pattern.

Front plain panel

Using yarn A, cast on 39 sts.

Row 1: Knit

Row 2: Purl

Rep rows 1–2 until work measures same length as Fair Isle panel from cast on edge, ending with a WS row.

Cast off.

To finish

BUTTON BAND

With RS facing and using yarn E, pick up and knit 88 sts along right-hand edge of Fair Isle panel.

Row 1: [K1, p1] to end.

Row 2: [P1, k1] to end.

These two rows form moss stitch.

Rep row 1 twice more.

Row 7: Moss 4 sts, cast off 2 sts [moss 11 sts, includes st used to castoff, cast off 2 sts] to last 4 sts, moss to end.

Row 8: Moss 4 sts, turn, cast on 2 sts, turn, [moss 11 sts, turn, cast on 2 sts, turn] to last 4 sts, moss to end.

Row 9: [K1, p1] to end.

Row 10: [P1, k1] to end.

Row 11: [K1, p1] to end.

Cast off in pattern.

With right sides facing, line up the left-hand edge of the plain panel with the pick up edge of the button band on the Fair Isle panel, so that the button band is lying on top of the plain panel. Use the position of the buttonholes to place the buttons correctly. Sew the buttons into place and then button them up to join the two panels.

Using the knitted cushion front as a template, cut backing fabric to size, allowing a 1.5cm seam allowance all the way around. Stitch the fabric to the cushion front. Insert cushion pad through button flap.

Creating inspiration

The hue family cushion on pages 150–153 demonstrates attention to value, proportion and stitchwork, with these elements highlighted by the envelope structure and choice of buttons. Successfully changing the colour palette of the project involves keeping the various elements balanced, even if they all change completely. These mood boards show you how we collected and arranged sources of inspiration to help us re-colour our cushion. Pages 156–157 show the knitted results.

Gold and purple variation

Nature is always a fantastic source of inspiration. The dried leaves and flowers of autumn provide a wealth of colours and encouraged us to look at the full spectrum available. In this mood board, although we have given much of the design over to a subtle blend of brown, gold and ochre, we have not forgotten the berry tone of damson.

Grey, blue and lemon variation

You may find that you are inspired by a collection of fabrics. You will see from the board below that we used a piece of fabric to set the feel for this reinterpretation and then added stationery, buttons, ribbon, etc to build up the range of colours. By highlighting certain colours in this way we were able to make our final yarn selection.

Beaded variation

Our final example was inspired by a piece of wallpaper. We wanted to create a really opulent piece and so decided to look for additional elements that were richer and darker than the original source. We added glamour by using beads, which also echo the bands of moss stitch patterning used in the hue family cushion. You will notice that lime green has been used sparingly to accent rather than overpower the combination of rich purple and chocolate brown.

Inspiration cushion variations

We used a hue family as the basis for our original cushion design, but what inspires you may be very different to what excites us. However, the principle of identifying your source and then exploring how it might be interpreted remains the same. The following variations show how we have reinterpreted the same cushion design and the principles used are ones you can apply to your own knit projects.

Gold and purple variation

We wanted to achieve a sense of mellowness with this piece. Our decision to blend a DK-weight yarn with a slightly darker, fine mohair and use a simple slip stitch pattern helps us to achieve a subtle finish. The Fair Isle section is much bolder, picking up on the tones of fallen leaves and highlighted with a berry-like purple for definition. Balance is achieved by working the moss stitch button band in the ochre colour found in the Fair Isle section and by adding textured buttons in similar tones.

MATERIALS

Yarn A = 2 balls of DK yarn

Yarn B = 1 ball of silk/mohair yarn
used double

Yarn C = 1 ball of DK yarn

Yarn D = 1 ball of DK yarn

Yarn E = 1 ball of DK yarn

FAIR ISLE PANEL

See chart.

STITCHWORK SECTION

Worked over 61 sts
as follows:

Change to yarn B.

Row 1: K2, yfwd, sl1, ybk [k1, yfwd, sl1, ybk] to last 2 sts, k2.

Row 2: Purl.

Change to yarn A.

Row 3: K3, yfwd, sl1, ybk [k1, yfwd, sl1, ybk] to last 3 sts, k3.

Row 4: Purl.

Rep last four rows three more times.

BUTTON BAND

Worked in moss stitch in yarn E.

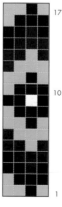

Grey, blue and lemon variation

The second variation moves from the mellow to the tranquil and uses a much 'cooler' palette. The garter stitch striped panels echo the interplay of blues found in our inspiration piece, while the Fair Isle section emphasizes how a different technique can impact on the way that we read colours. Focus is achieved with a dark blue garter stitch button band and shell buttons reflect our association of blue with water.

MATERIALS

Yarn A = 2 balls of
    DK yarn
Yarn B = 1 ball of DK yarn
Yarn C = 1 ball of DK yarn
Yarn D = 1 ball of DK yarn
Yarn E = 1 ball of DK yarn

FAIR ISLE PANEL

See chart

STITCHWORK SECTION

Worked over 61 sts
as follows:
Change to yarn B.
Row 1: Knit.

Row 2: Knit.
Change to yarn A.
Row 3: Knit.
Row 4: Knit.
Change to yarn D.
Row 5: Knit.
Row 6: Knit.
Rep rows 1–6 twice more
    and then rows 1–2
    once more.

BUTTON BAND

Worked in garter stitch in
    yarn C.

Beaded variation

Our third variation is the most dramatic. We have used gold beads instead of stitchwork to create a sense of glamour. The exuberance of the lime green mohair is underpinned by the more subtle use of blue-violet and dark brown patterning in the Fair Isle section. The dark brown is used again on the button band, providing a link with the Fair Isle and helping the blue buttons to sit comfortably alongside the beaded section.

MATERIALS

Yarn A = 2 balls of
    DK yarn
Yarn B = 1 ball of DK yarn
Yarn C = 1 ball of
    silk/mohair yarn
    used double
Yarn D = 1 ball of DK yarn
Approx 572 beads

FAIR ISLE PANEL

See chart.

STITCHWORK SECTION

Worked over 61 sts
as follows:

Row 1. K2, PB [k1, PB] to
    last 2 sts, k2.
Row 2: Purl.
Row 3: Knit
Row 4: Purl.
Row 5: K3, PB [k1, PB] to
    last 3 sts, k3.
Row 6: Purl.
Row 7: Knit
Row 8: Purl.
Rep rows 1–8 once more then
    rows 1–2 once more.

BUTTON BAND

Worked in moss stitch in
    yarn B.

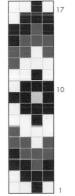

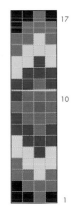

Abbreviations

A, B, C etc.	colours as indicated in the pattern	p	purl	tog	together
alt	alternate	p2tog	purl two together	WS	wrong side
approx	approximate(ly)	patt	pattern	yb	yarn back between needles
beg	begin(ning)(s)	psso	pass slipped stitch over	yfwd	yarn forward between needles
cm	centimetre(s)	rem	remain(ing)(s)		
cont	continue(s)	rep	repeat	yrn	yarn round needle
dec	decrease(s)	rev st st	reverse stocking stitch	*	repeat instructions between/following * as many times as instructed
DK	double-knitting	RH	right hand		
foll	follow(ing)(s)	RS	right side		
g	gram(s)	skpo	slip one, knit one, pass slipped stitch over	[ ]	repeat instructions between [ ] as many times as instructed
inc·	increase(s)	sl	slip		
k	knit	ssk	slip one, slip one, knit slipped stitches together through back loops		
k2tog	knit two together				
LH	left hand				
m	metre(s)	st st	stocking stitch		
m1	make one stitch	st(s)	stitch(es)		
mm	millimetres	tbl	through back loops		

Resources

UK

Rowan Yarns

Green Mill Lane

Holmfirth

West Yorkshire HD9 2DX

Tel: 01484 681881

www.knitrowan.com

Index

Acknowledgements

We would like to thank the following people who have all helped to make this book possible:

Thank you to Kate Buller at Rowan for allowing us to use their fantastic yarns and whose colours were a joy to work with. Thank you to Sharon Brant whose support and advice throughout this project has been invaluable. Thank you to the team at Collins & Brown and in particular Nina Sharman. Thank you to our photographers, Holly Jolliffe and Geoff Dann, who have really made the colours come alive and to Gemma Wilson for the great page design. We would also like to thank our wonderful knitters, Helen Tomes, Amanda Golland and Margaret (Sarah's mum). Lastly, we would like to convey a very big thank you to Kate Haxell whose wealth of knowledge and wonderful advice (not to mention calming influence!), helped us to make our dream book a reality.

A couple of personal thank yous.....

Emma would like to thank Jez, whose love and support she couldn't have done without.

Sarah would like to thank Paul and Phoebe for their love and encouragement throughout the project and always. Also her dad, who threaded beads and made sure her mum met her deadlines! And Emma, for inviting me to join her on this project and being such a good friend.

Love Crafts?

Keep updated on all exciting craft news from Collins & Brown

Register online at www.lovecrafts.co.uk for email updates on forthcoming titles